Dharma Tales for CEOs

Praise for *Dharma Tales for CEOs*

A wonderful book, where one can learn corporate affairs including management, governance and stories from the Puranas, Itihasas and other mythologies in parallel, and be able to connect the ethical and moral values. A must-read!

Rishabh C. Kothari, CEO of CKC Fragrances

The book's structure—featuring a prelude for each chapter, a story from mythology, a connection of the story to the corporate world, rapid-fire questions and a chapter summary—is incredibly innovative and enables quick comprehension of the concepts. One can easily finish the book while enjoying a mug of coffee!

V.K. Jhaver, chairman, Tropical Agrosystem (India) Pvt. Ltd

Hats off to Prakash for this short and crisp book that beautifully captures the dynamics of present-day corporates and the events in mythological stories, and connects them to bring a valuable learning of ethics and values. Kudos for this initiative, which will definitely pay off sooner or later.

A.L. Somayaji, former advocate-general of Tamil Nadu and currently senior advocate in Chennai

The book talks about understanding the larger cause of any event, focusing on high values, strategic thinking and, most importantly for the leaders, to show signs of humility and groundedness in relation to peers, employees and other stakeholders. A wonderful insight!

Rajmohan Pillai, bestselling author and chairman of Beta Group

The book covers major important corporate topics, but in very easy language, reaching a wider readership without losing the essence. I still wonder how the author managed to use such simple terms!

Sanjay Sehgal, chairman and CEO of MSys Technologies, angel investor and heartful human

Prakash's previous book and this one both emphasize how a leader should embody truthfulness, transcending the confines of traditionally accepted values in the modern world. I wholeheartedly recommend that this book be read, followed and, most importantly, embraced by leaders!

Kris Srinaath, former Indian cricketer, co-founder and CEO, S4Carlisle Publishing Services

If leaders and potential leaders grasp their shortcomings, take a moment to pause and reflect, read and comprehend this book, then engage in introspection regarding their leadership approach, I am confident they will recognize their own shortcomings and emerge stronger without fail.

Punit Lalbhai, executive director, Arvind Ltd

My heartfulness guru (Daaji) says that only spirituality can save this world. And Prakash reiterates this with the concept of spiritual quotient for leaders. Unless leaders develop and inculcate this, they cannot expect success, let alone climb up the ladder

R.R. Padmanabhan, international business coach and mentor

This book will indeed empower leaders to reach their fullest potential, as well as nurture those destined to become leaders.

M.K. Anand, founder of See Change and MSME evangelist

Dharma Tales for CEOs

BUSINESS TRANSFORMATION THROUGH Timeless Spiritual Principles

S. PRAKASH

HARPER BUSINESS

An Imprint of HarperCollins Publishers

First published in India by Harper Business 2024
An imprint of HarperCollins *Publishers*
4th Floor, Tower A, Building No. 10, Phase II, DLF Cyber City,
Gurugram, Haryana – 122002
www.harpercollins.co.in

2 4 6 8 10 9 7 5 3 1

Copyright © S. Prakash 2024

P-ISBN: 978-93-6213-921-4
E-ISBN: 978-93-6213-280-2

The views and opinions expressed in this book are the author's own and the facts are as reported by him, and the publishers are not in any way liable for the same.

S. Prakash asserts the moral right
to be identified as the author of this work.

All rights reserved. No part of this publication may be reproduced, stored in a retrieval system, or transmitted, in any form or by any means, electronic, mechanical, photocopying, recording or otherwise, without the prior permission of the publishers.

Typeset in 11.5/16.2 Garamond Premier Pro at
HarperCollins *Publishers* India

Printed and bound at
Thomson Press (India) Ltd

*To my beloved Daaji, Global Guide of Heartfulness;
my life partner, Sandhya, and my daughter, Sukanya;
and my teachers, coaches, business friends and acquaintances
from whom I have learnt a lot*

Contents

Foreword   xi
Preface   xv

1. Vision and Corporate Karma   1
2. Strategic Thinking and Dharma   14
3. Steadfast Execution and Personal Accountability   25
4. Great Communicator—Collective Upholding of Dharma and Swadharma   37
5. Altruism, or a Sense of Selflessness   49
6. The Interplay of Spiritual Quotient and Organizational Growth   61
7. Humility and a Sense of Groundedness   76
8. Guided by a Larger Purpose/Cause—The Unsolved Mysteries   90
9. Strong People Skills and Empathy   106
10. High on Values and Integrity: Dharma vs Swadharma   119

11. Baker's Dozen	135
12. A Bird's Eye View	155
Notes	167

Foreword

The primary focus of heartfulness is personal growth and spiritual development. Additionally, its principles and practices can also positively influence individuals in context of the business world. By integrating heartfulness practices into their lives, professionals can enhance their overall well-being, emotional intelligence, decision-making abilities, leadership qualities and creativity, leading to more fulfilling and successful career experiences.

I feel great joy in sharing this foreword for the remarkable second spiritual book for corporate sages (a.k.a. CEOs) of the modern era. *Dharma Tales for CEOs* reflects what I have mentioned earlier too: Integrating spirituality with materialism is crucial to the evolution of human beings. You cannot exclusively lead a materialistic life that will disable you at the spiritual level. If you delve excessively into spiritual life, you will become unproductive to society, yourself and your family. Like a bird flies with two wings, human life has to be carried on with two successful wings of life—material and spiritual.

The great modern-day saint and my spiritual teacher, Shri Ram Chandra of Shahjahanpur, taught us the significance of balance and harmony in all aspects of life. Shri Ram Chandra said: 'Spirituality is not in renouncing the world but in seeing divinity in every aspect of life ... The best way to love God is to love all, serve all.'

Accomplishing this does not have to involve complexity. He advocated simplicity and objectivity while satisfying the inner quest for spiritual growth. Today, reducing attachment to external possessions and focusing on inner growth and spiritual fulfilment is called being minimalistic and leading a sustainable lifestyle.

This book teaches readers how to serve humanity through the art of making profits while applying the principles and practices of spirituality. In a world filled with competition and pride, where the noise of a life loaded with electronics often drowns out the whispers of the soul, this book emerges as a gentle guide, offering values, wisdom, and a path to profound self-discovery. It acknowledges that CEOs are the new-age kings. As they explore the world of entrepreneurship, CEOs need an approach which reminds them that both dharma and swadharma coexist—an approach they will find within the pages of this book.

A CEO needs to embark on a transformative journey, one that transcends beyond the current state to the depths of inner consciousness, and take all others in the organization along with him.

You hold in your hands a treasure trove of profound insights, carefully curated and presented to awaken your innermost being. This book addresses themes of profit-making, wealth maximization, organizational growth and personal spiritual growth.

Today, global organizations are pursuing a triple-bottom-line approach, considering not only financial results but also positive human, social and environmental outcomes. CEOs are beginning to incorporate sustainable and responsible practices into their companies' operations by reducing their environmental impact, promoting employee well-being, supporting local communities and addressing social issues. An ordinary CEO can transform into a Spiritual CEO by recognizing and honouring the interconnectedness of individual and group goals, working towards a common purpose of enterprise-building guided by the highest values and ethics, and considering the broader impact of their actions on the world around them.

One way to do this is to align the principles of Environmental, Social and Governance (ESG) with the UN's Sustainable Development Goals (SDGs). This not only contributes to a better future for people and the planet, but also enhances brand reputation, attracts socially conscious investors, drives long-term business success and leaves behind a strong legacy of ethical business for the next generation.

Prakash's book promotes responsible practices throughout the business and corporate value chain—inspiring readers to deepen their connection with nature, understand interconnectedness, emphasize compassion and empathy, contribute positively to communities, engage in responsible practices and govern the stakeholders to live in alignment with the highest principles and values. This invaluable guide encourages maximizing the return from available resources with minimal waste. It depicts how one can generate joy by doing good business and in doing so create a lasting, sustainable legacy for future generations.

May your heart be open, your spirit be receptive and your soul be forever transformed.

Daaji
Global Guide of Heartfulness

Preface

The path to leadership is a journey rife with challenges and opportunities. Whether one holds the position of CEO in a multinational conglomerate or spearheads a fledgling start-up, there's an unceasing stream of situations demanding tough decisions, team inspiration and the upholding of ethical standards.

Within these pages lies a treasury of narratives rooted in ancient India, each a gem bearing lessons in performance, morality and ethics that resonate resoundingly even in modern times. These tales encapsulate timeless qualities and behaviours, rendering them universally applicable and relatable to individuals across diverse walks of life—a truth that endures to this day as they continue to be passed down generations.

Contained within this volume are carefully curated selections of dharma tales, each serving as a wellspring of insights into the realms of leadership, decision-making and ethical comportment, among other themes. Every story is accompanied by a reflection section, a spotlight on the central lesson it imparts, coupled with pragmatic guidance on its application within the context of contemporary business. These stories stand ready to assist CEOs in navigating intricate scenarios, fostering more profound connections with their teams, and rendering decisions in alignment with their core values and beliefs.

A steadfast conviction accompanies this endeavour, that this book shall emerge as a fount of inspiration and counsel, serving CEOs and leaders united in their aspiration to construct thriving enterprises imbued with integrity and compassion. May these narratives guide the readers, in the pursuit of their goals, to lead with sagacity, empathy and poise, even as they relentlessly chase numerical achievements.

Delving deeper, we encounter the concept of spiritual cognition, an integral facet for CEOs navigating the corporate labyrinth. This transcends the mere sensory and intellectual, venturing into the profound sphere of awareness that surpasses rational thought. This mode of knowing sheds light on reality's essence, life's purpose and the tapestry of existence itself—a reservoir of profound wisdom crucial to a CEO's sojourn within the corporate realm.

Spiritual cognition's contributions to a CEO's leadership journey abound. Primarily, it instils a profound sense of purpose, aligning the CEO's endeavours with a greater tapestry, and sustaining motivation even in times of adversity. This deeper purpose fosters resilience and unwavering dedication. Secondly, spiritual cognition cultivates heightened self-awareness, enabling CEOs to adeptly allocate their resources, identify strengths and weaknesses, and make decisions that are inherently beneficial to their companies and employees alike. Thirdly, this mode of perception engenders empathy and compassion, enabling CEOs to grasp the diverse perspectives of their teams and foster a harmonious work environment. Lastly, spiritual cognition bestows resilience upon CEOs, endowing them with inner fortitude and wisdom to navigate challenges with equanimity, fostering prudent decision-making even in turbulent times.

In essence, the teachings of dharma tales and the insights offered by spiritual cognition intertwine to shape a holistic approach towards leadership. The narratives speak of principles that endure through epochs, and spiritual cognition provides the means to internalize these principles and apply them effectively. As CEOs embark on their journey to lead with purpose, authenticity and compassion, these dual pillars serve as guiding lights, illuminating the path towards transformative leadership and organizational success.

Spiritual cognition emerges as a potent tool, offering CEOs a pathway to equilibrium amid the whirlwind of their leadership voyage. By cultivating an enriched sense of purpose, self-awareness, compassion and resilience, CEOs can metamorphose into more adept leaders, and architects of a harmonious and encouraging work milieu, fostering the growth and well-being of their employees.

The narrative consistently underscores the vital capacity of a leader to access their innermost reservoirs—a wellspring that transcends mere intelligence or emotional quotient. This profound well of insight serves as an unwavering anchor, fortifying a leader across the spectrum of circumstances. This truth resonates regardless of whether one dons the mantle of CEO or seeks to immerse themselves in the realms of leadership and personal advancement.

As the expedition into this literary realm commences, a gentle prompt arises—an invitation to approach each topic with an open, receptive mind, primed to embrace novel notions. Allow the subheadings to serve as wayfinders, guiding you towards unexpected revelations and illuminating paths that lead to insights hitherto unexplored.

This book's aspiration is to ignite the spark of intellectual curiosity within you, evoking a lifelong ardour for knowledge acquisition and fostering an insatiable quest for wisdom. Unified in this endeavour, let us embark upon an extraordinary sojourn through the ever-evolving, ever-enchanting tapestry of human insight.

And so, the stage is set for us to delve into the chronicles of yore—timeless tales brimming with lessons that remain as pertinent today as they were at their inception. As we traverse these narratives, may their resonance illuminate and guide you towards transformative and enlightened leadership.

1

Vision and Corporate Karma

yo māṁ paśhyati sarvatra sarvaṁ cha mayi paśhyati
tasyāhaṁ na praṇaśhyāmi sa cha me na praṇaśhyati

(For those who see Me everywhere and see all things in Me,
I am never lost, nor are they ever lost to Me.)
—Bhagavad Gita, chapter 6, verse 30

Context

One of the key defining qualities of a leader is vision, which, here, means a simple bold statement of the future; a lofty dream that makes everyone stretch themselves to achieve.

Setting forth a vision may be relatively easy, but keeping faith in that lofty goal, chasing it day after day while naysayers brand it as a 'pipe dream', is hard. Then, there's how to keep team members motivated. When we give up identifying with our small, limited selves, and instead, identify ourselves with the supreme self inside (an extension of God), our worldview expands exponentially. We begin to feel potent grace all around us. The seemingly impossible becomes doable and viable. Our divine possibilities shine over venues that we were blind to. The situation effortlessly falls into place as a higher power guides us towards supra-achievements.

Prelude

An indispensable trait that distinguishes a 'leader' is the possession of a lucid and resolute vision. The significance of a well-defined leadership vision is manifold.

First, it imparts a sense of direction, thereby bestowing unwavering clarity upon the team of followers. This is instrumental in guiding the concerted efforts of the team towards a shared objective.

Furthermore, a crystalline vision serves as a wellspring of motivation, sustaining the team's vigour throughout the crests and troughs of their journey. Such motivation often propels the team members to surpass their perceived limits, achieving feats beyond their initial estimations. When individuals can vividly envisage a vision that unveils a compelling and distinct future, they are predisposed to invest the extra effort required to actualize it.

However, the benefits extend beyond motivation; a vision significantly enhances the process of decision-making. By providing a framework for evaluating prospects and perils, a well-crafted vision empowers leaders and team members alike to make choices in consonance with their overarching long-term vision and goals.

Yet another advantage is the facilitation of communication. A clear vision serves as a beacon, enabling leaders to transmit their objectives and expectations to the team. It ensures that all stakeholders share a common understanding of their roles in contributing to the organization's triumph.

Moreover, a meticulously delineated vision functions as a benchmark, fostering accountability. With a shared comprehension of the vision, individuals can gauge their performance against it, thereby making necessary adjustments to ensure alignment with the desired outcomes.

Thus, a vivid leadership vision is indispensable for providing orientation, nurturing motivation and establishing a scaffold for decision-making, communication and accountability.

Beyond the realm of mundane visions lies an aspiration that transcends—a spiritual vision. Typically encompassing a profound, meaningful experience, a spiritual vision is often perceived as transcending the bounds of the conventional, material world. It frequently entails a sense of connection to something grander than the self, such as a divine or universal force. This spiritual insight entails heightened awareness of one's emotions and thoughts, and a deeper comprehension of the interdependence of all existence. These spiritual visions can offer profound insights into the nature of reality and one's role within it. They can also serve as fountains of inspiration, counsel and healing for those fortunate enough to experience them.

When fused with a materialistic vision, the inclusion of a spiritual dimension equips a leader to reap the benefits from both realms. This synthesis enhances the leader's capacity to steer the organization towards greater heights by harnessing the synergies of diverse perspectives.

The following narrative will illustrate the interconnections that unite the threads of this story, with the theme of clear vision and corporate karma.

Bhishma and the Bed of Arrows

The Mahabharata war is being fought and the Pandavas are not able to make many breakthroughs. They know for sure that until Bhishma, the 'Pitamaha' (literally 'grandfather', also used for great-uncles like him) of the Pandava and Kaurava cousins, is removed, they will not be in a position to win the war.

Following Lord Krishna's strategic advice, the Pandavas place Shikhandi between Arjuna and Bhishma. An intriguing story from Shikhandi's past life as Amba emerges, wherein Shikhandi was a woman named Amba who had suffered deeply at the hands of Bhishma. Having departed with a vow to seek revenge, Amba is born a woman and transitioned to man named Shikhandi. When they are positioned before Bhishma in the midst of battle, Bhishma realizes that he cannot release even a single arrow, stemming from his perception of Shikhandi, because he sees not their current life but the past existence where he had wronged them. Thus, when Arjuna fires arrows from behind Shikhandi, Bhishma is unable to defend himself.

Finally, when Bhishma falls, he lands upon a bed of arrows. All of Pandavas and Kauravas gather around. Subsequently, Bhishma decides to invoke the boon bestowed upon him, enabling him to choose the moment of his demise. He selects the fifty-eighth day from then, which would be the winter solstice at the conclusion of Dakshinayana (literally 'south-bound Sun', i.e., winter) and the commencement of Uttarayana (literally 'north-bound sun', i.e., spring). Throughout this period, he engages in introspection, attempting to fathom why, despite his lifelong commitment to honesty and candour, must he endure such profound suffering, with numerous arrows penetrating his body, making a literal deathbed. Regrettably, he fails to unearth an answer, despite his grasp of how dharma and karma intricately intertwine. Reflecting on around seventy-two previous existences, he remains unable to pinpoint a compelling rationale for his current circumstances. It is at this juncture that he beseeches Lord Krishna for assistance.

'Bhishma, you are only blessed to see up to seventy-two lives,' Lord Krishna clarifies, and then shows him one of the lives prior to that. In that life, Bhishma is riding his chariot, hunting or fighting someone. There is an insect which keeps bothering him, and with one swat, he gets that insect killed and thrown out of his way. When he does that, the insect falls into a bush of thorns, and its body is apparently pierced with a thousand thorns. The effect of this karma had been lying dormant, awaiting fructification in a suitable environment, which arrived in this life, on the battleground of Kurukshetra. Naturally, people are intrigued and start asking Lord Krishna why Bhishma had to wait for so many lives.

Lord Krishna unveils two truths. He explains that the initial rationale lies in the fact that throughout the span of those lifetimes, Bhishma led an exceedingly virtuous existence, characterized by unwavering adherence to values. This virtuousness reached such an elevated level that there existed no conceivable path through which this particular karmic consequence could have manifested or borne fruit. However, in the context of his present life, the conditions were ripe for it to manifest.

Once again, the gathering asks Krishna why this manifestation occurred in this specific life. He responds that in this life, Bhishma had chosen silence in the face of numerous tribulations endured by the Pandavas, particularly the harrowing ordeal suffered by Draupadi. Notably, he remained passive during the disgraceful incident in which Draupadi was subjected to humiliation within the kingdom's halls during the gambling episode, as the Kauravas attempted to disrobe her. Bhishma's lack of action in this instance acted as the catalyst for unfurling the effects of that previous karma, which he has to endure in this very existence.

Relationship Between Dharma and Karma

Now, I would like to present a series of questions that you need to truly internalize and deeply contemplate, in order to arrive at a resolution. The incident involving Bhishma and the insect illustrated a deliberate action on his part. Now, envision the countless instances when we simply walk and inadvertently crush insects, worms and other forms of life. What implications might arise from nature, or result as a consequence of these actions? Consider the multitude of bacteria that we unknowingly eliminate during basic bodily functions like breathing and digestion. For now, you can set this consideration aside, as we will revisit the narrative of Bhishma's story in due course.

Indeed, it is an incredibly captivating narrative that reveals a complex interplay not only between our held values, but also between our actions and the intricate interweaving of karma and dharma. These forces, when combined, can either lead to tumultuous consequences, or give rise to the experiences individuals must endure.

The narrative prompts us to grapple with a pivotal question: What precisely constitutes the relationship between karma and dharma? Can alterations in our karmic equations influence our perception of dharma? Could a mere solemn vow, such as Bhishma's commitment to safeguarding the Kaurava clan, hinder his capacity to maintain his forthrightness when it was imperative, even amidst the tribulations faced by the Pandavas at the hands of the Kauravas?

There are many such dharmic questions which actually come up in the story. It is for us now to analyse and find—as a potential ruler of a nation, head of an organization or head of a family, and as a family member—what are the dharmic equations. What are the values that the story teaches us? Why did Bhishma have to go through this sorry state of affairs, even though Lord Krishna himself pointed out all the good he had done in the seventy-two lives prior? What do we really learn? When do we allow the karma to interfere in dharma, and when do we ensure that the karma actually unfolds in such a way that dharma can be made to be upheld, which is what is essential for holding up the universe?

There is so much to debate and so much to learn. Please contemplate what are the dharmic equations we can learn here—there are multiple ones present. What do we learn from this to avoid the mistakes of the people in the story, whether it was Bhishma, Shikhandi, Arjuna or any of the Pandavas who got entangled in this? How do we ensure that dharma is upheld, however virtuous you are in this life?

Here are some of the dharmic equations that warrant contemplation:

Impact of unconscious actions: Reflect on how seemingly small, unconscious actions can have far-reaching karmic consequences.

Ethical predicaments: Consider the ethical dilemmas that leaders face when deciding between personal dharma and universal dharma.

Interplay of karma and dharma: Contemplate the intricate relationship between karma (actions) and dharma (duty), and how they intertwine to shape one's destiny.

Value of inaction: Ponder the consequences of remaining silent or inactive in the face of injustice, and how such choices can impact one's dharma and karma.

Resonance in leadership: Analyse how Bhishma's story mirrors the challenges a leader encounters, where ethical choices impact duties and roles.

Conscious living: Explore the concept of conscious living and its implications on the ethical and karmic dimensions of one's actions.

Balancing dharma and karma: Delve into the complexities of balancing one's duty with the consequences of past actions, seeking alignment with universal principles.

In various potential leadership roles, it's essential to internalize the lessons encapsulated within Bhishma's story. Delve into the intricacies of dharma and karma, acknowledge the ramifications of passivity, and reflect upon the far-reaching effects that individual choices can have on the intricate tapestry of the universe. By delving into these profound concepts, you can foster a heightened comprehension of ethical decision-making, and the profound repercussions it holds for leadership and life in its entirety.

How This Tale Connects to the Corporate World

The old adage 'life is what unfolds while we are busy planning' encapsulates a profound truth. Bhishma's story puts subtle emphasis on the imperative to navigate the middle path between the success of an organization in the material world, and the reverberations of its past and present actions on its present and future trajectory. While we may conceive compelling corporate visions, destiny often beckons us toward an uncharted course, amid the unfurling of 'corporate karma'—a continuum that links our past and present.

Corporate karma underscores the notion that a company's actions can cast ripples of positive or negative consequences onto its future. This concept is rooted in the belief in the cosmic equilibrium, asserting that virtuous deeds will be rewarded, while transgressions will face retribution—applicable both to personal lives and corporate landscapes. Although empirical evidence might not decisively validate the existence of corporate karma, it is pivotal to recognize that not all phenomena yield to scientific scrutiny. For some, corporate karma serves as an explanatory framework delineating the variance in success levels among companies; for others, it acts as a catalyst encouraging ethical and responsible corporate conduct.

To fathom the depths of corporate karma, the concept of cause and effect warrants exploration. The axiom 'you reap what you sow' remains resonant even in the contemporary context. The influence of a company's actions on its future, whether positive or negative, is incontrovertible. Entities distinguished by ethical and responsible conduct tend to draw in customers, employees and investors. Conversely, those branded as unethical and irresponsible confront the prospect of boycotts, legal action and regulatory scrutiny.

Moreover, the realm of a leader's vision is not immune from the influence of corporate karma. Leaders who subscribe to the notion of corporate karma exhibit a proclivity for decisions aligned with the organization's best interests and stakeholder welfare. Additionally, they are poised to cultivate an environment characterized by positivity, ethics and empathy.

In the landscape of leadership, corporate karma instils a reminder: that success is not solely a product of strategic acumen and profit generation; it is an amalgamation of ethical choices, responsible actions and a commitment to nurturing an environment that fosters growth and well-being. The tapestry of corporate karma underscores the interconnectedness of actions, consequences, and the profound interplay of destiny and intention. It serves as a moral compass, urging companies and leaders to weave their narratives with threads of integrity, compassion and forward-looking responsibility.

If leaders are conscious of the impact of corporate karma, they are likely to:
- Make decisions that are in the best interests of the company and its stakeholders. For example, they may be more likely to invest in environmental sustainability or social responsibility initiatives.
- Create a positive and ethical work environment. For example, they may be more likely to promote diversity and inclusion, or to create a culture of respect and trust.
- Attract customers, employees and investors who share their values. This can lead to increased sales, productivity and innovation.

Corporate karma can be a powerful force for good in the world. When companies act in an ethical and responsible way, they can create a more just and sustainable world.

Questions that Matter

What role does spirituality play in shaping a corporate vision?

Spirituality is a broad term that can be defined in many ways. For the purposes of this discussion, we will define spirituality as a sense of connection to something larger than oneself, such as a higher power, nature, or the universe. Spirituality can play a significant role in shaping a corporate vision, as it can provide a sense of purpose and meaning beyond simply maximizing profits. A spiritual perspective can help a company identify its values and mission, and guide its decision-making processes. This can lead to increased employee engagement, productivity and innovation.

Ultimately, the role of spirituality in shaping a corporate vision is to create a workplace where employees feel connected, inspired and motivated. When employees feel this way, they are more likely to give their best work and help the company achieve its goals.

How can a company incorporate spiritual values and beliefs into its mission statement and core values?

Incorporating spiritual values and beliefs into a company's mission statement and core values can bring about a sense of purpose, ethical grounding and holistic well-being in the workplace. By acknowledging the importance of spiritual aspects and aligning them with business practices, a company can foster a positive organizational culture that values both individual growth and collective success. It needs a deliberate and intentional effort. You need to start with a clear understanding of the company's spiritual values. What are the core beliefs that guide the company's actions? What are the values that the company wants to promote in its workplace? Once the company has a clear understanding of its spiritual values, it can begin to incorporate them into its mission statement and core values.

How can a company promote and encourage spiritual growth and development among its employees?

Promoting and encouraging spiritual growth and development among employees can enhance their well-being, foster a positive work environment, and ultimately, benefit the company's bottom line. Here are some ways a company can promote spiritual growth and development among employees:

Foster a sense of community: Create opportunities for employees to connect with one another and build a sense of community. This might include team-building activities, group outings, or regular staff meetings where employees can share their thoughts and ideas.

Provide personal development opportunities: Offer training and development opportunities that encourage personal growth and development, such as leadership workshops, coaching sessions or personal growth retreats.

Embrace diversity: Embrace diversity and encourage employees to learn from each other's spiritual and cultural backgrounds. This can help create a more inclusive and supportive work environment and foster a sense of belonging among employees.

How can a company balance the need for profits with a commitment to spiritual principles and values?

Balancing profits and spiritual principles involves integrating ethical decision-making and holistic well-being into business practices. Implement transparency, fair trade and sustainable practices to align with spiritual values. Develop products/services that benefit both society and the environment. Encourage ethical leadership that values empathy, integrity and social responsibility. Prioritize employee well-being through heartfulness/mindfulness programmes, flexible schedules and growth opportunities. By fostering a values-driven culture and embracing long-term sustainability, a company can harmonize profit goals with spiritual principles, contributing positively to both its bottom line and the well-being of stakeholders.

Chapter Summary

- To truly lead, a leader must possess a clear organizational vision that guides and steers through various challenges.

- Once the vision is established, sharing it with the team fosters enduring motivation throughout the ebbs and flows of the journey.
- Embracing a spiritual vision allows leaders, organizations and teams to connect with something transcendent and universal, fostering a perception of interconnectedness among all things.
- Harmonizing both material and spiritual visions equips the organization (leaders and team) to harmonize diverse influences, thereby maintaining focus even during difficult times.
- More importantly, it empowers leaders to strike a harmonious balance between karma and dharma.
- The adoption of a spiritual vision contributes to the smoothing of corporate karma, bringing equilibrium and harmony.

2
Strategic Thinking and Dharma

vasamsi jirnani yatha vihaya
navani grhnati naro 'parani
tatha sarirani vihaya jirnany
anyani samyati navani dehi

(Like a person puts on new garments and gives up old ones, the soul accepts new material bodies, giving up the old and useless ones.)

—Bhagavad Gita, chapter 2, verse 22

Context

Adapting new strategies and shunning older ones is among the biggest secrets to success in any business. But learning to adapt to the changes quickly is a key factor for any leader. Don't get stuck with your old strategies. Lord Krishna mentions that even the human soul gives up a useless body. Thus, business leaders must learn to explore, and live like a traveller who doesn't get attached to a city or place of visit, but instead, enjoys the experience.

Prelude

Strategy is a critical component of effective leadership. Leaders who prioritize strategic thinking are better equipped to navigate complex challenges, seize opportunities and drive their organizations toward long-term success.

Much like vision, strategy serves as a guiding light, illuminating the path ahead. It possesses the power to unite everyone under a shared objective. A meticulously crafted strategy articulates the organization's identity, its aspirations and the roadmap to attaining those aspirations. This tactical framework aids leaders in discerning what holds paramount importance, and in making judicious choices regarding resource allocation. Furthermore, it furnishes leaders with the nimbleness required to navigate shifts in the business landscape. Through anticipation of potential hurdles and the formulation of contingency plans, leaders can pivot swiftly, circumventing unforeseen setbacks.

Moreover, a lucid strategy plays a pivotal role in harmonizing stakeholders—employees, investors and partners—around a shared vision, culminating in heightened engagement and motivation. It operates on the foundation of quantifiable objectives, allowing leaders to chart progress and gauge achievements. Through vigilant tracking of key performance indicators, leaders can identify areas that need refinement, and flexibly modify their strategy in response.

In essence, strategy emerges as a linchpin for effective leadership by providing direction, channeling focus on to priorities, fostering agility, aligning stakeholders and facilitating progress assessment. By placing strategic contemplation at the forefront, leaders set their organizations on a trajectory towards continuing success, realizing their objectives with heightened efficiency and efficacy.

It's imperative to delve into another facet—how dharma can significantly influence strategic thinking. Dharma is a multifaceted concept in Hinduism and other Indian religions, generally signifying the principles or duties governing human conduct and morality. Its impact on strategic thinking is profound, as it underscores the significance of ethical action and adopting a long-term perspective.

One manner in which dharma can mould strategic thinking is by urging leaders to prioritize the well-being of all stakeholders, transcending short-term profits or gains. Dharma can also mould strategic thinking by endorsing the notion of karma, wherein actions bear consequences that ripple beyond immediate circumstances. Moreover, dharma can propel leaders to approach challenges with detachment and equanimity, rather than being entangled in emotions or ego.

Collectively, dharma can furnish a valuable framework for strategic thinking that accentuates ethical conduct, a long-range outlook and a commitment to the broader welfare.

Krishna, Bhishma and the Death of the Pandavas

Let us look at a very interesting and powerful story from one of the climactic episodes of the Mahabharata war, involving Bhishma, Krishna and Draupadi. This will help us to learn about strategy, and the impact of dharma on it.

As we cast our mind to Kurukshetra, the battle is getting intense and Duryodhana cannot find an edge over the Pandavas, as he expects to. It is evident that Lord Krishna is successfully executing his plans.

Duryodhana, getting frustrated, decides to talk to Bhishma, the commander-in-chief of the Kaurava army, and raises suspicions about the 'Pitamah'. Without respect or courtesy, even for his age, he tells Bhishma: 'You love the Pandavas very much and that is precisely why we are not winning this battle.'

He finally pushes Bhishma into taking a vow—that by the next evening, either he or the five Pandava brothers will stay alive. And we all know Bhishma is capable of delivering on his vow—after all, he got the name Bhishma because of it. The old man marks five arrows and says: 'These are the five arrows which are going to kill the Pandavas.' Duryodhana wants to be sure, so he even picks up the arrows and walks out, just in case Bhishma would change his mind.

On the other side, Lord Krishna senses this and knows that if Bhishma has taken a vow, he is bound to fulfil it. Therefore, he goes to meet Draupadi and seeks her help to nullify this vow—he works tactically to ensure that the Pandavas' interests are taken care of. He tells Draupadi curtly that the Pandavas are dead, leaving her—their wife—startled and upset. She then asks Lord Krishna: 'What do you mean the Pandavas are dead? How can you make such a statement?'

Krishna responds: 'I didn't make that statement, it is Bhishma who has vowed this.'

Draupadi knows this means serious trouble, and doesn't really know what to do. Then she falls at the feet of Lord Krishna and says: 'Please tell me what needs to be done now.'

Krishna devises a strategy and tells her: 'Come along with me, let's go to the battlefront where Bhishma is resting for the night.'

Krishna disguises himself as a servant, knowing that the guards outside Bhishma's tent will not allow him to enter, as on the battlefield, there are rules and guidelines in force. However, he also knows that there is an exception to the rules—women and old people are allowed to visit. So, the guards let Draupadi in, but stop Krishna outside Bhishma's tent.

Now, Draupadi doesn't know what to do. Krishna, looking into the tent from a distance with his divine vision, gives her a workable plan—he tells her to just sneak in, touch Bhishma's feet quickly and ask for his blessings. He also warns her clearly to be extremely careful, because her actions will determine the future of battle the following day.

Holding her breath, she slowly moves in. As she reaches Bhishma's tent, she literally crawls; Bhishma is in deep sleep. She goes near the foot of his bed, touches his feet and says: 'Please bless me.'

Bhishma instantly awakes and thinks it is Duryodhana's wife Bhanumati who has come to take his blessings. He blesses her, saying '*deergha sumangali bhava*', which is a blessing for the woman to remain married; i.e., for her husband to have a long, healthy life.

Soon after, when he looks at the woman whom he has blessed, Bhishma is shocked to find it is Draupadi, not Bhanumati. So, now, he has vowed two things—that he'll kill the Pandavas, and that the Pandavas' wife will lead a long married life. This is where the battle of dharma really starts.

Bhishma angrily says to her: 'I know for sure that you would not have come alone, and I am very sure that there is somebody behind you.' Draupadi tells him that she has a servant who has come along, to which Bhishma says, 'please show me who the servant is'. He tells the guard to get the servant in, and when the disguised Krishna walks in, Bhishma recognizes him as the Lord himself, falls at his feet and asks: 'Why have you done this?' Krishna and Bhishma then have a long conversation, where the former explains whatever he can to the latter.

In the meantime, Duryodhana plans to replace Bhishma with Karna as the commander of his troops, irrespective of whether his grandfather successfully kills the Pandavas or gets killed by them. That's the way he wants the battle to go, and the whole thing unfolds accordingly.

The Dilemma Between Means and Ends

In real life, there are often two or more warring factions, each of which wants to win the battle. In this situation, how does dharma unfold? Did Bhishma's vow, made in front of Duryodhana, come to have an impact in the story? He also made a commitment to Draupadi.

Lord Krishna, being the adviser to the Pandavas, had to pull off something miraculous to ensure that they wouldn't be killed, and would go on to win the battle. For him, the ultimate dharma was to keep the Pandavas alive.

Whether you are a CEO of an organization or heading your nation, there are multiple factions and questions that arise. 'What should I do in this situation? Do the means justify the end, or does the end justify the means, bypassing or compromising dharma on the way?' Lord Krishna did what he felt was right; Bhishma had to stick to what he had committed to Draupadi, which contradicted his initial commitment to Duryodhana.

How does this learning apply to our daily lives? Do we encounter situations where, in the pursuit of our desires, we sometimes bend the rules? Do we adopt a holistic perspective on dharma? Or do we, in the pursuit of upholding dharma's ultimate goal, find ourselves making compromises? Is such an approach equitable or justifiable? Does the fact that the Lord himself adopted such a stance mandate that every one of us must follow suit? Did Bhishma inadvertently overlook his dharma?

This story presents us with captivating and potent questions that span a spectrum of choices, igniting thought-provoking discussions.

How This Tale Connects to the Corporate World

This story provides a classic illustration of dharma ultimately overshadowing strategic thinking. In the corporate context, it's often equated to 'values/ethics'. The adage 'values must precede strategy' holds true. While many organizations merely pay lip service to this principle, only a handful take it seriously. If your strategy isn't aligned with dharma, the outcomes are significantly influenced by dharma, not just strategy. Despite looking impressive on paper, why do strategies frequently fall short of translating into results? Is it solely due to poor execution, or does it stem from poor dharma at the outset?

In this narrative, we will delve into the realization that Duryodhana and the Kauravas had their strategies formulated, but their critical misstep (not just here, but throughout the Mahabharata) lay in failing to harmonize strategy with dharma. While it may appear tactical, what Krishna did by bringing Draupadi to seek Bhishma's blessings on that fateful night exemplifies dharma seamlessly aligning with strategy, granting the Pandavas a strategic advantage at every stage of a war that was heavily skewed against them.

Dharma, in essence, can be understood as the 'right path of action'. A leader guided by dharma makes decisions that serve the best interests of all stakeholders: the organization, its employees, customers and the broader community. Regardless of whether we acknowledge the link between dharma and our thought processes (strategic and otherwise), it functions. This rests on the universal principle that a 'lack of understanding of a concept or truth doesn't negate its operation in this world'.

Let us see a few situations in how dharma tends to impact strategic thinking; specifically for those who innately abide by the concept of dharma.

They tend to consider the impact of their decisions on all stakeholders: When making decisions, a leader who is guided by dharma will take into account the impact on all stakeholders, not just the organization itself. This means considering the needs of employees, customers and the community at large.

They tend to make decisions that are ethical and sustainable: This means making decisions that are fair and just, and do not harm the environment.

They work towards building a strong and ethical culture: This means creating a culture where employees feel valued and respected, and where they are encouraged to do the right thing.

Questions That Matter

How can incorporating spiritual practices or beliefs enhance strategic thinking in a corporate setting?

Spiritual practices are activities or rituals that individuals engage in to connect with their inner selves, a higher power, or a sense of transcendence. These practices aim to foster a deeper understanding of life's meaning, promote personal growth and cultivate a sense of peace and well-being. Strategic thinking refers to the cognitive ability to analyse complex situations, anticipate future developments and devise well-considered plans of action to achieve long-term goals.

If you can see the link, you will realize it looks paradoxical—spiritual practices are more inward-looking, whereas strategic thinking is more outward-looking. The real connection between the two comes from the juxtaposition of the inward journey helping shape the outward thinking, and that is precisely where these two find convergence.

What are some spiritual practices or principles that can be applied to strategic planning and decision-making by incorporating the values of dharma?

Dharma is a central concept in Hinduism, Buddhism and other Eastern religions that refers to cosmic order, righteousness and duty. Applying the values of dharma to strategic planning and decision-making can help individuals align their actions with their deeper sense of purpose and meaning. By incorporating the values of dharma into strategic planning and decision-making, businesses can create a more ethical and responsible workplace, and can make decisions that are more likely to benefit all stakeholders.

How can a company encourage its employees to develop their spiritual awareness to improve their strategic thinking abilities?

Encouraging employees to develop their spiritual awareness can be a powerful way to enhance their strategic thinking abilities and promote their overall well-being. By integrating spiritual awareness into the workplace, a company can empower employees to approach strategic thinking with a deeper understanding of themselves and their broader purpose. This holistic approach can lead to more thoughtful, compassionate and effective decision-making that benefits both, individuals and the organization.

What are some potential challenges or obstacles that may arise when incorporating dharma into strategic thinking, and how can they be overcome?

Dharma is a complex and multifaceted concept, and it can be challenging to incorporate it into strategic thinking in a way that is both meaningful and effective. Incorporating dharma into strategic thinking can bring many benefits, but there are also potential challenges and obstacles that may arise. Here are some examples of potential challenges and how they can be overcome:

Overemphasis on personal spiritual growth: One potential challenge is that individuals may become too focused on their personal spiritual growth, and lose sight of the organization's goals and mission. This can be overcome by emphasizing the importance of aligning personal growth with the organization's goals and values.

Resistance to spiritual concepts: Another challenge is that some individuals may be resistant to spiritual concepts, and may view them as irrelevant or unimportant in a corporate setting. This can be overcome by providing education and resources on the benefits of spiritual practices, and by showing how they can enhance strategic thinking and overall well-being.

Lack of support from management: Furthermore, some individuals may feel that they lack support of the management to engage in spiritual practices or develop their spiritual awareness. This can be overcome by providing leadership training that emphasizes the importance of spiritual awareness, and encouraging managers to model spiritual practices and values themselves and chart out their own path.

Overall, incorporating dharma into strategic thinking can bring many benefits, but it requires careful attention to potential challenges and obstacles. By emphasizing alignment with organizational goals and values, providing education and resources and fostering a culture of support and inclusiveness, these challenges can be overcome, and individuals can develop their spiritual awareness and enhance their strategic-thinking abilities.

Chapter Summary

- An effective strategy must be established to align all stakeholders toward a shared objective.
- Strategy empowers leaders to concentrate on priorities and fosters adaptability in response to the ever-evolving demands of the industry or market they operate within.
- The organization's values epitomize its dharma, which, when aptly envisioned, harmonizes with the crafting of strategies.
- When leaders and the management team integrate dharma with mindfulness—a state of being fully present and attuned to the present moment—it engenders heightened clarity and concentration. This, in turn, aids in the formulation of robust and effective strategies.
- When solid values (dharma) are firmly in place, concerns about ultimate outcomes dissipate, enabling undivided focus on the process (strategies) with unwavering energy and time. This dedicated pursuit invariably guides one towards optimal results.

3

Steadfast Execution and Personal Accountability

karmaṇaiva hi sansiddhim āsthitā janakādayaḥ loka-saṅgraham evāpi sampaśhyan kartum arhasi yad yad ācharati śhreṣhṭhas tat tad evetaro janaḥ riya pramāṇaṁ kurute lokas tad anuvartate

(By performing their prescribed duties, King Janak and others attained perfection. You should also perform your duties to set an example for the good of the world. Whatever actions great people perform, common people follow. Whatever standards they set, all the world pursues.)

—Bhagavad Gita, chapter 3, verse 20-21

Context

Leaders of a company have a moral responsibility to set lofty examples of responsibility/accountability, and inspiring the rest through their words, deeds and character. When noble leaders are at the forefront, the rest of the company naturally gets uplifted in morality, selflessness and spiritual strength. But in times when there is a vacuum of principled leadership, the rest of the firm has no standards to pursue, and slumps into self-centeredness, moral bankruptcy and spiritual lassitude. Hence, great leaders should always act in an exemplary manner to set the standard for the world.

Prelude

Steadfast execution and personal accountability are concepts that are closely intertwined. Steadfast execution entails consistently and diligently pursuing tasks or objectives, without becoming distracted or losing focus. Personal accountability involves assuming ownership of one's actions and their consequences, and taking responsibility for the outcomes they produce. These two qualities are crucial for anyone aspiring to succeed in any domain. When your execution remains steadfast, you commit to seeing your objectives through to completion, regardless of the challenges that arise. Simultaneously, personal accountability entails acknowledging and assuming responsibility for both actions and results.

These qualities are interdependent, constituting a commitment to fulfil promises and accept responsibility for the results achieved. When individuals personally hold themselves accountable for their actions, they are more likely to execute tasks and attain their goals with unwavering consistency and discipline. This heightened sense of accountability stems from their recognition of the influence their actions exert, and an understanding that their choices carry repercussions.

Conversely, the absence of personal accountability can impede steadfast execution. Individuals may struggle to maintain focus on their goals or honour their commitments when they are not fully invested in the outcomes. This lack of commitment can foster tendencies like procrastination and avoidance, which erode the ability to execute tasks consistently and with discipline.

In summary, personal accountability emerges as a pivotal factor in achieving steadfast execution. When individuals take ownership of their actions and the resulting outcomes, they position themselves to accomplish tasks and objectives with enhanced focus and discipline.

We are going to look at one of the most interesting stories in the Mahabharata—of a valiant warrior who gave his life for the cause. This is the story of Abhimanyu; his birth, his growth, how he met his death, and the various perspectives of the people in this story. Does the end justify the means, or are the means more important than the end?

Abhimanyu and the Chakravyuha

Abhimanyu was the son of Arjuna, the third Pandava brother, and Subhadra, the sister of Lord Krishna. At the time Abhimanyu was conceived, Lord Krishna had shared with Arjuna how to enter the Chakravyuha—a tactical army formation designed to deceive the opponent, trap them inside and kill them. Subhadra was also present and listening, as was the foetus Abhimanyu in her womb.

Lord Krishna then revealed to Arjuna the way to win if the enemy presented the Chakravyuha. It is said that when the Mahabharata war started, on the Pandavas' side, Krishna and Arjuna were the only two people who had complete knowledge of it. Lord Krishna, who knew the future, also understood very well that Abhimanyu would have to be there on that day to fight the war.

Abhimanyu, in spite of his courage, valour and whatever victories he was to get on the day he entered the Chakravyuha, was not supposed to get out of it. And hence, Krishna, very subtly, lulls Subhadra to sleep, which ensures that the foetus Abhimanyu does not hear the second half of his explanation—how to get out of the Chakravyuha. This was part of the Lord's mega plan. There is also a twist in the story, which I will reveal later.

When the Pandavas were exiled for thirteen years, Subhadra, with her young son, decided to stay back with her brothers Krishna and Balarama. In these formative years, Abhimanyu was taught the best warfare techniques by Krishna and Balarama, which made him a strong and valiant warrior.

Fast forward to the war in Kurukshetra. The first ten days are all about Bhishma and the Pandavas, before Bhishma falls. From the very next day, the Pandavas begin losing steam, especially Arjuna, who goes into despair about the impending death of his favourite great-uncle Bhishma, at his own hands, and doesn't know how to get out of this trauma. As usual, Lord Krishna has to cook up a plan to ensure that Arjuna comes roaring back.

While Krishna is planning how to get Arjuna out of this funk on the twelfth day of the war, on the other side, Duryodhana is working out the best way to finish off the Pandavas with the help of Dronacharya and Karna, who has now entered the battlefield. They realize it is difficult to defeat Arjuna and the other Pandavas; in fact it is far beyond their own scope, especially after the great warrior Bhishma lay on the bed of arrows. So, they decide that the best way to achieve their goal is to do what one would do in a game of chess— corner the leader of the other side, Yudhishthira, the true follower of dharma, and take him into custody or, better yet, kill him.

Dronacharya comes up with a master plan to deceive Arjuna and take him in an altogether different direction, engaging him in war elsewhere, and then targeting Dharmaraj, i.e., Yudhishthira. In the Kaurava's view, only Krishna and Arjuna know how to get in and out of the Chakravyuha, and with Krishna not actively fighting the war and Arjuna distracted elsewhere, they think the job is done. And their plan does go very well, except for one thing—they haven't accounted for Abhimanyu entering the fray.

As the Kaurava side is organizing the Chakravyuha, Abhimanyu suddenly takes the lead and tells his paternal uncles that he knows how to get in. Yudhishthira and the other Pandavas know very well that Abhimanyu will only be able to get in, but not get out. They decide to enter the Chakravyuha along with Abhimanyu and fight their way out, so as to ensure that they all get back.

As the battle unfolds and they near the entrance of the Chakravyuha, the Kauravas' sole brother-in-law Jayadratha comes out and stops the four Pandavas, ensuring that only Abhimanyu gets trapped. As Abhimanyu enters, the Chakravyuha closes behind him, and he realizes he cannot get out, because only his father and maternal uncle know how to exit it. But he still valiantly kills one warrior after another—some of the foster brothers of Karna, the children of Duhshasana, and one of the sons of Duryodhana.

Throughout the war up to this point, the battles were fought one on one, but the furious Kauravas then break the rules of dharma and decide to attack Abhimanyu simultaneously. Ashwathama, Duryodhana, Dushyadhana, Shakuni, Karna and Dronacharya all come together to attack the sixteen-year-old, and yet, he bravely takes them on and goes on a killing spree. Eventually, Karna angrily breaks Abhimanyu's bow, but he still doesn't give up and fights with a mace or whatever else he can find. Now, Ashwathama closes in, and slowly he gets all the other weapons Abhimanyu has at his disposal.

Abhimanyu finds himself backed into a corner, encircled by these colossal warriors, who audaciously assail him collectively, discarding all established tenets of warfare. Nevertheless, what he does do is seize a cartwheel and continues to wage the battle. This time, they all dismount and unsheathe their swords, assaulting him from every angle, culminating in Abhimanyu's death.

Now, to the twist that I had mentioned earlier. How many of you are aware that Abhimanyu was a reincarnate of Varchas, son of the moon god, Chandra? When the gods wanted the son to take birth on earth and be part of the Mahabharata, the moon god said: 'I love my son too much; I cannot be without him for long. Even if I have to send him, I will send him only for sixteen years.' And that, apparently, was one of the reasons he was killed at that age. Lord Krishna was fully aware of this.

See how things unfolded? Krishna deliberately allowed Arjuna to be taken out of the war, because his plan was to infuriate Arjuna at the death of Abhimanyu. This is exactly what happens over the final five days of the war, which Arjuna and his brothers win.

How to Deal With a Breach of Trust

Undoubtedly, the emotions and sentiments evoked by this narrative are overwhelming, and are not just limited to the story of Abhimanyu and the Chakravyuha. How often have we encountered feelings of betrayal and experienced the breach of trust by our own family members, close associates or relatives? Doesn't it occur in the workplace as well, where we're disappointed by those we trusted—be it our dependable team members or even our superiors?

A warrior who valiantly stood for dharmic principles ended up sacrificing himself, but ensured that his paternal uncles were saved. Lord Krishna achieved his objective, and Duryodhana still went ahead and lost the main cause of the battle—belief in his right to the throne—which he was trying to turn to his advantage. This is a fantastic dharmic value—right from his conception, Abhimanyu learnt all kinds of warfare for just one single day—the thirteenth day of the Mahabharata war. The climax of the thirteenth day is a culmination of multiple facets of a beautiful dharmic war.

What lessons can we learn from this scenario? Was Lord Krishna's decision to ensure Abhimanyu's demise driven by the belief that it would galvanize Arjuna to give his utmost, or did it align with a commitment that Abhimanyu was destined to reunite with his father, the moon god Chandra? These captivating questions are capable of sparking limitless discussions. What intricate ethical considerations are at play here? Do we encounter such intricate dilemmas in our day-to-day existence, within the corporate realm, and even in the governance of nations? In situations where opposing factions collide, individuals are often sacrificed as pawns, and the ultimate objective overshadows the methods employed, these scenarios offer fertile ground for multifaceted analyses. Allocating a few moments for contemplation on these facets is truly worthwhile.

What moral principles underlie Abhimanyu's killing? What messages did Lord Krishna aim to convey? What reflections might have occupied the thoughts of Dronacharya and Duryodhana? How does this situation harmonize with the preservation of dharma? What insights can we glean from it? This narrative presents a treasure trove of lessons, which we can delve into through careful and contemplative exploration.

How This Tale Connects to the Corporate World

Abhimanyu exemplified steadfast execution by fearlessly charging into battle with determination. Unwavering and resolute, he focused on his goal, executed his plan with discipline and showcased unwavering resolve.

Despite recognizing his vulnerable position, he placed the cause of the war above his own safety. While he executed his role effectively, his support team fell short. Despite insurmountable odds, Abhimanyu refused to yield, or compromise his dharma. He fought valiantly and boldly, steadfast in his duty and committed to upholding his family's honour. In his battle, dharma stood as his ally, infusing him with the strength and bravery necessary to confront his adversaries. Even in his final moments, Abhimanyu remained faithful to his dharma, steadfast in his refusal to surrender or compromise his principles.

Ultimately, Abhimanyu's story illustrates the significance of both execution and personal accountability in attaining success. The path to our aspirations requires disciplined execution and focused determination, coupled with an inherent responsibility for our personal growth and development, enabling us to confront any challenges that arise.

While this story is not an endorsement of risking one's life for work, it exemplifies an extreme instance of commitment to dharma and personal ownership (partially of one's swadharma) over outcomes. Consider the brave soldiers who defend our borders—they are aware that the odds stacked against them, and yet they are driven to fulfil their mission, even if it entails sacrificing their own lives.

It serves as a reminder that in the face of adversity, maintaining focus on our goals and persevering is crucial. Similarly, the demise of one individual does not signify the end of the struggle. A few departures from an organization (even if they are high performers) should not greatly impact its long-term trajectory. With determination and courage, even the most daunting challenges can be surmounted.

In the realm of corporate leadership, the tale of Abhimanyu metaphorically underscores the value of personal accountability. Leaders must be prepared to acknowledge their errors and take responsibility for their actions. They must also be willing to learn from their mistakes, and make adjustments to prevent recurrence. Leaders should stand up for their convictions, even when it's arduous. They must be ready to champion their employees, customers and shareholders.

Above all, the narrative conveys that leaders should be inspiring figures, motivating their teams to attain greatness. They should instil a sense of purpose, and the belief that individual contributions can effect meaningful change in the world.

The saga of Abhimanyu serves as a compelling reminder that leaders should embody strength, courage and accountability. Remember that people tend to emulate what they observe, rather than what they are told. When leaders embody these attributes, they inspire their teams to achieve remarkable feats.

Questions that Matter

How can leaders and managers use spirituality to inspire and motivate employees to take ownership of their work and goals?

Leaders and managers can leverage spirituality by creating a purpose-driven and values-aligned environment. Here's how:

Connect work to higher purpose: Help employees see how their tasks contribute to a larger purpose or mission that aligns with spiritual values. Highlight the positive impact they can make.

Provide autonomy: Empower employees to make decisions within their roles. This autonomy fosters a sense of ownership and responsibility.

Provide resources: Offer resources such as mindfulness workshops, meditation spaces and reading materials to support employees' spiritual growth.

Recognize individual growth: Acknowledge employees' personal and professional growth journeys. Celebrate milestones that align with their spiritual development.

Provide mentorship: Pair employees with mentors who exemplify spiritual and values-based leadership, guiding them to take ownership of their paths.

Foster a culture of trust and collaboration: Leaders and managers can foster a culture of trust and collaboration, where employees feel safe to take ownership of their work, and contribute to the organization's goals.

Embrace diversity: Honour diverse spiritual beliefs and practices, fostering inclusivity and a sense of belonging among employees.

Celebrate successes and show appreciation: Leaders and managers can celebrate successes and show appreciation for employees' contributions, which can inspire a sense of pride and ownership over their work and goals.

How can a company hold employees accountable for their actions while also promoting a supportive and empathetic culture?

Holding employees accountable for their actions and promoting a supportive and empathetic culture can seem like conflicting goals, but it is possible to do both. Here's how a company can achieve this:

Set clear expectations: Companies should set clear expectations for employees, including values, goals and standards of behaviour. When expectations are clearly communicated, employees are more likely to understand what is expected of them, and are more likely to hold themselves accountable.

Encourage open communication: Companies should encourage open communication, where employees feel comfortable sharing their concerns or mistakes. This helps to create a supportive and empathetic culture, while also promoting accountability.

Build culture of learning from mistakes: When employees feel safe admitting errors, they are more likely to take responsibility for their actions.

Use a restorative justice approach: This approach focuses on repairing the harm caused by a mistake, rather than simply punishing the employee. By encouraging employees to take responsibility for their actions and make amends, the company can promote a supportive and empathetic culture, while still holding employees accountable.

Celebrate successes: Companies should celebrate the successes and accomplishments of employees, which promotes a positive work environment and encourages employees to take ownership of their work.

By emphasizing clear communication, empathy, recognition and a collaborative approach, a company can effectively balance accountability and a supportive, empathetic culture. This fosters a positive work environment where employees feel motivated to take ownership of their actions, while knowing they have the backing of a caring organization.

Chapter Summary

- Empowering leaders and teams with accountability directly contributes to the resolute execution of the mission.
- Holding leaders and teams accountable fosters a sense of ownership and responsibility within them.
- This, in turn, cultivates elements of innovation and entrepreneurship in their missions and tasks.
- Over time, this nurtures emerging leaders and teams and nudges them to boldly step up and shoulder accountability and responsibility for the next critical mission.
- The fusion of accountability and steadfast execution infuses them with qualities of discipline and wisdom, enabling optimal resource utilization and delivering excellence.

4

Great Communicator—Collective Upholding of Dharma and Swadharma

*anudvega-karam vākyam satyam priya-hitam cha yat
svādhyāyābhyasanam chaiva vān-mayam tapa uchyate*

(Words that do not cause distress, are truthful, inoffensive and beneficial, as well as regular recitation of the Vedic scriptures—these are declared as the austerity of speech.)
—Bhagavad Gita, chapter 17, verse 15

Context

Leaders often stand out for their ability to communicate effectively. The power of expression ranks as a fundamental requirement for a successful executive. In this verse, Lord Krishna imparts to Arjuna the refined art of communication. It's worth noting that Arjuna is a prince, so Krishna's guidance applies to contemporary executives as well. According to the Gita, the following constitute the cornerstones of proficient communication:

- It should avoid stirring agitation in the listener's mind.
- It must refrain from igniting base emotions within the listener.
- It must convey the truth.
- It should be beneficial to the listener.
- It should please the ear.
- Such communication should only be undertaken after thorough self-analysis.

Upon close examination of these principles, we can be assured that these qualities are precisely what can render the communication of present-day executives remarkably effective.

Prelude

Effective communication from a leader—regarding values, dharma, swadharma, karma, vision and strategy—is indispensable in cultivating a robust team that collaborates towards shared objectives.

Values serve as guiding principles, shaping the behaviour and choices of a team. When leaders communicate these values transparently, it enables team members to comprehend expectations and synchronize their actions with the overarching mission of the organization.

Dharma encompasses the duties and obligations individuals bear towards themselves, their community and the world. A leader can emphasize the significance of dharma to the team, fostering a sense of purpose and significance in their roles.

Swadharma (one's own dharma) refers to an individual's distinct responsibilities or duties. While dharma constitutes the natural law governing the universe, swadharma represents each individual's distinctive role in upholding this law—it embodies how one contributes to society's greater welfare. Swadharma isn't predetermined; it's a personal process of discovery. It emerges through reflection upon one's unique talents, capabilities and passions, while considering society's needs and one's potential to address those needs. Living in harmony with swadharma results in a dharmic life, marked by peace, happiness, and fulfilment, aligned with natural law and societal welfare.

Karma pertains to the repercussions of one's actions. When leaders communicate about karma, it enlightens team members about the impact of their deeds on the organization, and the broader world. This understanding motivates responsible conduct and ethical decision-making.

Vision and strategy stand as pivotal elements in any prosperous organization. Leaders must communicate these aspects to the team, ensuring clarity on objectives, and everyone's role in contributing towards them. This alignment fosters a collective endeavour towards a shared target, facilitating enhanced success.

In essence, a leader's adept communication on values, dharma, swadharma, karma, vision and strategy is pivotal to constructing a resilient and cohesive team united in pursuit of common goals.

The concept of collectively upholding dharma suggests that within a community or organization, all individuals share the responsibility of adhering to dharma. It's insufficient for only one person to act ethically or fulfil their duties; the entire group must do so for the community or organization to thrive.

For instance, in a business context, the collective upholding of dharma entails that ethical and responsible behaviour is upheld by all employees, not just senior executives. Each individual contributes to upholding the organization's values, and when all play their part, the company can operate with integrity and achieve sustainable success.

Likewise, in a family setting, collectively upholding dharma implies that every member has a role in promoting the family's well-being. Parents must fulfil their responsibilities towards their children, and children must show respect to their elders and contribute positively to the family.

Essentially, collectively upholding dharma involves group members recognizing their duties and acting for the greater good. When this approach is embraced, communities and organizations can flourish, achieving their objectives harmoniously.

The Maharishi and the Dog

In this story, we will delve into the significance of collective adherence to dharma within a society, forming a cohesive moral fabric. For the sake of clarity, consider the 'warp' of the fabric as an individual's functioning, and the 'weft' as representing the larger society—both intertwining to uphold dharma. This process contributes to maintaining the unity of the universe. Furthermore, we'll explore how effective communication assumes a paramount role in achieving this endeavour.

Many readers would be acquainted with the concept of Agyatvasa in the Mahabharata. For those who aren't, allow me to provide a concise introduction: Agyatvasa refers to the year the Pandavas spent living incognito after their initial twelve-year exile. The stipulation was that if any of their identities were exposed during this year, they would be subjected to an additional twelve years of exile in the forests.

On one of the days in the Agyatvasa, when the Pandavas were in the forest, they happened to meet the sage Narada, commonly known as the apparent creator-of-confusions wherever he goes, and also a staunch bhakt of Lord Vishnu, who keeps chanting 'Narayana, Narayana'. But as we'll see, the confusions he apparently creates lead to a positive solution, clarity and wisdom.

Yudhishthira, the eldest of the Pandavas and called Dharmaraj for his commitment to and prowess in dharma, had a series of interesting conversations with Narada, with the view to refine himself further.

'How shall I lead my personal life? How do I live my life as a king? By what values and what dharma should I actually lead myself and lead—or leave—the kingdom as well?' Yudhishthira asks.

'O Yudhishthira, instead of giving you a direct answer, let me share a story with you,' says Narada. 'And from this story, you may be able to make out what it means to lead your personal life, your interpersonal life, and how to rule as a king when you have a court, subjects and ministers.'

Narada shares the story of a Maharishi (sage) who lived in the forest. Through meditation and penance, the Maharishi develops a special power of attracting animals towards him. The animals feel a lot of peace in his presence. So, wherever he is in his ashram, all kinds of animals come near him, feel the peace, and then go away.

Somehow, a dog lands up in the ashram, and begins staying near the Maharishi. One day, when the Maharishi is meditating, a fierce-looking leopard walks into the ashram, and the dog is terrified. It immediately runs into the lap of the Maharishi, who understands what the dog is going through. Out of his love and compassion for this animal, the Maharishi thinks he'll give something to the dog to make it feel comfortable. Through his yogic powers, he turns the dog into a leopard.

The dog-turned-leopard now goes to the forest, and with its new power, starts terrifying other small animals. Then, one day, it meets a tiger, which is obviously more powerful. Like its previous incarnation, the dog-turned-leopard starts shuddering again, and runs back to the ashram and into the lap of the Maharishi. The Maharishi understands what has happened, and turns the dog-turned-leopard into a tiger.

With this new power, the dog-turned-tiger goes back into the forest, and lives without fear until it meets a bigger animal, an elephant. Now, it runs back to the ashram and into the Maharishi's lap, shuddering again. The Maharishi now turns the former dog into an elephant.

This creature now lives happily and roams freely around the jungle, until it sees an eight-headed demon—supposedly the most powerful creature in the forest in those days. Scared again, the dog-turned-elephant runs to the Maharishi, who now turns him into the eight-headed demon.

With its new power, the dog-turned-demon goes back into the forest and thinks it is its new king. It starts terrifying smaller creatures as well as people, and one day, it starts thinking: 'Now I am the most powerful... How would it be to tease, frighten and consume the Maharishi himself?' This, he thinks, will be the ultimate test of its strength and power.

The moment this thought crosses the creature's mind, the Maharishi's yogic powers immediately inform him of what it is thinking, and the sage turns the demon back into a dog. The dog then returns, falls at the feet of the Maharishi and starts crying, begging his pardon.

Narada ends the story here, and Yudhishthira learns his lesson. Let us go into the details of what he learnt.

How This Tale Connects to the Corporate World

In the world of business and leadership, the term 'Great Communicator' often transcends mere eloquence or charisma; it embodies the profound ability to inspire collective action and uphold the principles of Dharma and Swadharma. Within the context of organizational dynamics, a Great Communicator serves as a catalyst for aligning individuals with a shared sense of purpose and ethical responsibility, fostering a culture where each member recognizes and embraces their unique contribution to the greater whole.

In this book, the exploration of the Great Communicator archetype delves deep into the significance of nurturing a collective commitment to Dharma and Swadharma within corporate environments. Through anecdotes, insights, and practical wisdom, this narrative emphasizes the pivotal role of communication in reinforcing values, fostering trust, and ultimately, propelling organizations toward sustainable success rooted in integrity and authenticity.

The story vividly illustrates the connection between upholding dharma and swadharma on the one hand, and leadership communication on the other.

In this story, the Maharishi's act of granting the dog's wishes signifies the broader significance of adhering to dharma and individual swadharma. While the dog may pursue its own desires or objectives, it cannot infringe upon the overarching dharma, which would be to infringe upon the rights of other animals in the forest. There is a designated place for everything and everyone within the grand scheme of the universe. Although temporarily an individual's swadharma (real or perceived) might seem to surpass the greater dharma, leaders must ensure that dharma takes precedence over swadharma.

Leaders, as the Maharishi exemplified, must strike a balance between individual and collective aspirations, finding an equilibrium between swadharma and dharma.

Now, let me pose a few questions:

- How do you perceive this story from the perspective of a king, a subject, an individual or someone with a family?
- Have you encountered individuals with such values? Do you encounter individuals who consistently take from you without offering equivalent worth?
- What unfolds when you grant what they seek?

Furthermore, let's delve into additional inquiries to expand and refine our intellect and perspectives:

- How do the story's elements translate into dharmic and swadharmic values?
- What inquiries arise from the narrative?
- What responses do these inquiries elicit?
- When confronted with people who primarily take from you, how do you manage and respond?

As you begin to provide for them, and they amass power, a similar pattern emerges, reminiscent of political systems worldwide. When you vote for individuals who solicit or manipulate votes, and they acquire power, what unfolds in the subsequent years? These questions warrant introspection.

Now, let's apply these reflections to corporate life. Suppose you are within a corporate setting, and delegate executive authority to an employee, who then misuses it and returns to try and assert influence over you. What dharmic and swadharmic queries arise from this? How would you address them? How can reevaluating the concept of dharma aid in reinforcing the moral fabric of the universe (in this case, your organization), ensuring it remains cohesive as it should be?

Questions that Matter

What spiritual principles or practices can be used to enhance communication skills and foster effective communication among employees, and by extension, to its board and its customers?

There are several, of which I'm listing a few here:

Mindfulness and heartfulness: Mindfulness is the practice of being fully present and aware of the present moment. By cultivating mindfulness, individuals can become more focused and attentive listeners, which can lead to more effective communication. Mindfulness can also help individuals regulate their emotions and stay calm during difficult conversations. Likewise, heartfulness helps people transform, allowing them to listen more empathetically, based on the heart too, rather than just the mind.

Active listening: This involves not only hearing what others are saying, but also truly understanding their message. This requires individuals to listen attentively, ask clarifying questions, and reflect on what they have heard to ensure that they have understood correctly.

Presence in meetings: Encourage being fully present in meetings—mindful participation promotes meaningful contributions and reduces distractions.

Listening circles: Create opportunities for employees, board members and customers to engage in 'listening circles', where individuals share their thoughts and concerns in a supportive environment.

Non-violent communication: This is a technique that focuses on expressing feelings and needs without blaming or judging others. By using nonviolent communication, individuals can avoid misunderstandings and defensiveness, and create a more positive and productive conversation.

Storytelling: Encourage the use of storytelling to convey messages and values. Storytelling captures attention, makes information relatable and fosters connections.

Heartful speech: This is the practice of using words carefully and intentionally. By choosing one's words carefully, individuals can avoid misunderstandings and ensure that their message is clear and effective.

By integrating these spiritual principles and practices, organizations can create a communication culture that is respectful, empathetic and meaningful. This approach not only enhances relationships among employees, the board and customers, but also contributes to a positive and harmonious work environment.

How does leadership communication enhance the collective upholding of dharma?

This can be done by promoting a shared understanding of dharma among team members, and creating a culture that supports its principles. Dharma, as mentioned earlier, is a Sanskrit term that refers to a set of moral and ethical principles that govern human behaviour and guide individuals towards righteousness and virtue.

Leaders who communicate effectively and embody the principles of dharma can inspire their team members to follow in their footsteps. This can lead to a collective commitment to upholding dharma in the workplace and in other areas of life.

Moreover, leaders who demonstrate integrity, honesty and transparency in their communication can inspire trust and respect among team members.

What are some real-life examples of Indian companies that have successfully integrated spirituality into their communication practices, and achieved better business outcomes as a result?

Here are a few examples, based on my interactions and observations:

Tata: One of India's largest conglomerates, the Tata group has a long tradition of incorporating spirituality into its business practices. This includes the practice of corporate dharma, which is based on the principles of integrity, ethics and social responsibility. The group's leaders have emphasized the importance of these principles in their communication and decision-making, which has helped build trust and respect among employees and customers.

Wipro: The leading IT services company has incorporated mindfulness practices into its leadership development programmes. This includes meditation and other mindfulness exercises that help leaders cultivate focus, emotional intelligence and self-awareness. This has led to improved communication and collaboration among team members, and better decision-making.

Mahindra & Mahindra: This diversified conglomerate has incorporated spirituality into its business practices through its 'Rise' philosophy. This is based on the principles of respect, integrity and sustainable development. The company has communicated this philosophy to its employees and customers through its advertising campaigns and other communication channels, which has helped to build a strong brand reputation.

Heartfulness Institute: While not a traditional company, the Heartfulness Institute, having its roots in ancient Indian spiritual wisdom, has impacted individuals and organizations through its spiritual and heartfulness programmes. Many professionals and companies have integrated these practices to enhance employee well-being, stress management, and overall performance, while pursuing their individual spiritual beliefs.

These examples demonstrate that integrating spirituality into communication practices can lead to improved employee engagement, ethical decision-making, enhanced customer relationships, and a positive impact on the bottom line. By fostering a values-driven culture, these companies have not only achieved better business outcomes, but have also contributed positively to society and stakeholders.

Chapter Summary

- Open, transparent and clear (OTC) communication from leaders and management establishes the framework and foundation for team members to emulate and bridge gaps.
- OTC communication also sows the seeds of trust between team members and leaders, which, when nurtured consciously, fosters faith.
- Spirituality enriches communication with the essence of dharma.
- OTC communication fosters a sense of unity throughout the organization.
- It also significantly diminishes the misuse of power and the exploitation of challenging times by a few greedy individuals, thanks to the strength of a larger, aligned collective.

5

Altruism, or a Sense of Selflessness

tasmād asaktaḥ satataṁ kāryaṁ karma samāchara
asakto hyācharan karma param āpnoti pūruṣhaḥ

(Therefore, perform your prescribed duties without attachment. One who acts unattached to the results attains the supreme.)

—Bhagavad Gita, chapter 3, verse 19

Context

Leaders hold a significant responsibility—that of delivering the promised results to their executives and shareholders. However, an excessive fixation on results alone can often create a cutthroat atmosphere within corporate environments. In such scenarios, employees might find themselves lacking motivation to prioritize ethical actions, and perceive self-interest in the leader's motives. If leaders can showcase, through their conduct, that their service to the company transcends personal gain—such as their compensation, organization's scale or political influence—it can inspire a selfless approach among others in the organization. This infusion of selflessness into corporate life can foster a lasting perspective on organizational well-being, and cultivate a stronger allegiance to corporate values.

Prelude

Altruism is the practice of showing selfless concern for the well-being of others, encompassing acts of kindness and generosity without expecting any reciprocation. On the contrary, leadership involves motivating and guiding others towards a shared objective.

While these two concepts may initially appear at odds, there exists a robust connection between altruism and effective leadership—altruistic leaders typically excel in motivating and inspiring their teams. By giving precedence to the needs and interests of their team members, such leaders cultivate an environment of trust and allegiance that ultimately leads to enhanced performance and positive outcomes.

Furthermore, leaders who give prominence to altruism tend to be viewed as ethical and reliable which, in turn, bolsters their credibility and influence. Additionally, they are more inclined to foster a workplace culture that promotes positivity, and where team members feel esteemed and supported. This conducive atmosphere often brings forth facets of individuals that are customarily reserved for their personal spaces.

In summation, although leadership and altruism are different, they are intricately intertwined. Leaders who manifest a sense of selflessness and prioritize the well-being of their team members invariably prove to be more adept and influential in their leadership roles.

While the impact of altruism on the preservation of dharma and the advancement of an organization could hinge on the specific context and interpretation of these concepts, a robust correlation certainly exists between selflessness, ethical principles and organizational triumph.

King Shibi and the Dove

Many individuals have inquired why I choose stories from the past, rather than contemporary ones. I tell them I select stories that provide a platform for meaningful debate and substantial learning about dharma and enduring moral values. These narratives withstand the test of time and remain relevant across generations. Naturally, in due course, when appropriate contemporary narratives become available, I assure you that I will also embrace them for analysis and discussion. We must embark on this journey with open minds and open hearts, aiming to unearth the invaluable pearls of wisdom embedded in the tales of our ancestors and our cultural heritage.

Now, I'm going to touch upon a very interesting story—of a king, Shibi, known as the epitome of fairness, justice and dharma, not just towards his human subjects, but to all animals and creatures in his kingdom. Beyond references in Hindu texts and Buddhist scriptures like the Jataka tales, King Shibi is also said to have connections with the legends of the later Chola dynasty.

King Shibi is sitting in his court when a dove comes flying in and sits on his lap. The dove looks frightened for its life, so, in his kindness, King Shibi asks what is the problem. The dove says: 'O King, I am being chased by a hawk.' Shibi says: 'Don't worry, I will give you protection'.

At that moment, the hawk chasing the dove also flies into the courtyard and tells the king: 'Please allow the dove to go, as it is my prey, and it is only natural justice that I must be allowed to satiate my hunger. Neither do I disturb you, nor anyone else.'

Shibi listens patiently to the hawk and says: 'Though whatever you're saying is apparently true, the dove has taken refuge in me, and I have given a commitment that I will protect it.'

The hawk says: 'You're a fair and just king. You're supposed to be taking care of justice from all sides. You have given protection to it, which means you're denying the food which is due to me. Please give me justice too. How am I going to alleviate my current hunger?'

King Shibi thinks this through, and tells the hawk: 'I can feed you anything you want.'

The hawk says: 'Since you have given refuge to this dove, I want you to give your own flesh—as much as the dove weighs—and I will go away.'

The king finds this a fair argument, and orders his staff to bring a weighing scale, and cut a portion of his flesh that is equal to the weight of the dove.

Enduring the physical pain, and with blood oozing forth, King Shibi allows his flesh to be cut and weighed. However, to his and everyone else's surprise, the weighing scale does not get balanced. The king keeps on cutting more flesh out of his body, but nothing seems to work on the scale. Finally, with all humility, Shibi goes and sits on the weighing scale, saying: 'If this balances the scale, may it be so.'

Magically, as soon as he sits, the scale falls into balance. At this moment, the dove and the hawk turn into the fire god Agni, and the king of the gods, Indra, respectively. They say: 'We wanted to demonstrate to the world how just and fair a king you are. You have really demonstrated and delivered justice and dharma masterfully by protecting the dove, and at the same time, not ignoring the hawk.'

How the Tale Connects to the Corporate World

In this story, the hawk could've seized the dove had it been outside the king's protection. So, one may think that King Shibi denied the hawk its rightful sustenance. But when Shibi offered his own flesh to the hawk, what sort of dharmic values was he showcasing? What dharmic principles can we glean from the weighing scale balancing out once Shibi sat on it, even though the dove wasn't truly heavy? Next, can we identify individuals in the present era who hold such profound dharmic values—people who govern the nation, manage the state, lead an organization or guide a family? Would you desire such a leader in your life? Does this narrative hold deeper lessons for each of us—to be equitable, just and steadfast in following dharma in all our actions?

The tale of Shibi teaches us that upholding dharma isn't always straightforward, and might necessitate significant personal sacrifices. However, by doing so, we can garner the admiration and respect of others, and eventually, even the favour of the divine.

The story certainly holds relevance for the corporate world, particularly the role of the CEO, often seen as the leader and decision-maker of a company. Here are a few ways in which the narrative can be related to the role of a CEO in today's corporate landscape:

Sacrificing personal gains for the greater good: **Shibi was willing to sacrifice his own flesh to save the dove. Similarly, a CEO may need to sacrifice personal gains, such as bonuses or salary increases, for the greater good of the company and its stakeholders. This may involve making difficult decisions, such as cutting costs or laying off employees (even those performing well, but who are on the wrong side of the company's values), to ensure the company's long-term sustainability.

Encouraging altruism and empathy: A CEO can encourage these qualities by promoting a culture of collaboration, teamwork and social responsibility within the company. This can include implementing programmes that support charitable causes, fostering a positive work environment, and recognizing and rewarding employees who exhibit altruistic behaviour.

Balancing competing interests: King Shibi had to balance the competing interests of the hawk and the dove, and ultimately ensured that justice was served. Similarly, a CEO must balance the interests of various stakeholders, including shareholders, employees, customers and the wider community. This may require making difficult decisions and finding creative solutions that satisfy the needs of all parties involved.

Shibi's tale can serve as an inspiration for CEOs to lead with integrity, empathy and a clear sense of purpose, ultimately generating a positive impact on both the company and society at large.

Questions that Matter

How can one build a culture of 'giving back'?

Here are three steps to build such a culture:

Encourage others to give back: Talk to your friends, family and colleagues about the importance of giving back and serving others. Share stories of people who have made a difference in the world, and inspire others to do the same.

Make it easy for people to give back: There are many ways to give back, so make it easy for people to find ways to get involved. Provide information about local organizations that need volunteers, or create a matching gift programme that encourages employees to donate to charity.

Celebrate the accomplishments of others: When people give back, acknowledge their efforts and celebrate their accomplishments. This will encourage others to continue giving back and making a difference in the world.

How can a company encourage its employees to prioritize the needs of others while also achieving its business objectives?

Though it is challenging, encouraging employees to prioritize the needs of others while achieving business objectives requires a balanced approach that aligns personal growth, societal impact and organizational success. Here's how a company can achieve this:

Incorporate social responsibility into the company's mission and values: A company can clearly articulate its commitment to social responsibility by incorporating this into its mission statement and values. This can help employees understand that the company prioritizes serving others and giving back, even while pursuing business objectives.

Create a positive work environment: When employees feel like they are valued and respected, they are more likely to be motivated to help others.

Recognize and reward employees for their contributions: The company can recognize and reward employees for their contributions by giving them public praise, giving them a raise or bonus, a plaque or other award. The company can also create a 'giving back' award that recognizes employees who go above and beyond to help others.

Impactful projects: Provide opportunities for employees to work on projects that directly benefit communities, the environment, or social causes. These projects align personal growth with societal impact.

Align business objectives with social responsibility: Companies do this by setting goals that benefit both themselves and the community. For example, a company might set a goal of reducing its environmental impact or providing job training for disadvantaged youth.

Make giving back a part of the company culture: Companies can do this by providing employees with opportunities to give back through matching gift programmes, volunteer days or other initiatives.

Recognize and reward employees for their giving: Companies can recognize and reward employees for their giving by providing public recognition, bonuses, or other incentives.

Empower employees to make decisions: Both the company and the community can benefit if employees are given the authority to make decisions about how to allocate resources and prioritize projects.

Encourage employees to think creatively: Companies can encourage employees to think creatively about how to meet the needs of others by providing them with opportunities to brainstorm solutions to problems and come up with new ideas.

By encouraging employees to prioritize the needs of others, companies can create a more positive and productive work environment, improve customer service, enhance their reputation, and strengthen their community ties.

By implementing these strategies, a company can encourage its employees to prioritize the needs of others while also achieving its business objectives, creating a workplace culture that is both socially responsible and successful.

How can a company balance the need for profits with a commitment to giving back and serving the community or society they operate?

This requires a strategic and thoughtful approach that aligns business goals with social impact. Here's how a company can achieve this balance:

Integrate social responsibility into the company's business model: A company can do this by identifying ways to create value for both the company and the community. This can include investing in sustainable practices, reducing waste and carbon emissions, and creating products and services that benefit society.

Develop a social responsibility strategy: A company can develop one of these to identify key areas for investment, and outline a plan for achieving social impact. This can include setting targets for charitable giving, volunteering and community engagement.

Engage stakeholders: A company can engage stakeholders, including customers, employees and community members, in social responsibility initiatives. By soliciting feedback and input from these groups, a company can ensure that its social responsibility initiatives are aligned with its needs and priorities.

Measure and report social impact: A company can measure and report its social impact to demonstrate its commitment to giving back, and serving the community. This can include tracking metrics such as charitable giving, volunteer hours and environmental impact, and reporting on these metrics in an annual sustainability report.

Ethical business practices: Ensure that business operations uphold ethical standards. Prioritize transparency, fairness and responsible practices in all aspects of the company.

Impactful partnerships: Collaborate with nonprofit organizations, NGOs or community groups that align with the company's values and goals. Partnerships can amplify the impact of social initiatives.

Environmental responsibility: Incorporate sustainable practices that benefit the environment while aligning with the company's social responsibility goals.

Flexible giving models: Implement giving models that adapt to business performance. For example, allocate a percentage of profits to community initiatives, or tie 'giving' to specific product sales.

Long-term perspective: Embrace a perspective that recognizes the positive impact of community service on the company's reputation, customer loyalty and overall sustainability.

Community input: Involve local communities in identifying their needs and priorities. This ensures that the company's initiatives genuinely address community concerns.

Is it sincerely possible to pursue altruism and selflessness in this tough and competitive world?

Yes. While it can be challenging, there are many examples of individuals and organizations that have successfully incorporated altruistic principles into their work and lives.

The key is to recognize that pursuing altruism and selflessness does not mean ignoring the realities of the competitive world we live in. Rather, it means finding ways to integrate these principles into our work and lives in a way that supports both our own success and the well-being of others.

There are many benefits to pursuing altruism and selflessness, including increased happiness, improved relationships and a sense of purpose and fulfilment. Additionally, organizations that prioritize social responsibility and community engagement often experience greater customer loyalty, employee satisfaction and long-term financial success. It is altruism that helps create building a lasting legacy in this world, as history keeps telling us repeatedly.

Here are some examples of how we can pursue altruism and selflessness in our own lives:

- Volunteer our time to help others in need.
- Donate money to charity.
- Be kind and compassionate to everyone we meet, even those who are different from us.
- Stand up for what we believe in, even if it is unpopular.
- Forgive those who have wronged us.
- Be grateful for what we have, and not take it for granted.

Ultimately, pursuing altruism and selflessness requires a commitment to balancing our own self-interest with the well-being of others. It is a journey that requires ongoing reflection, learning and growth, but the rewards are worth it for both individuals and organizations that choose to take this path.

Several companies, both Indian and foreign, have successfully integrated spirituality into their culture, achieving business success while cultivating a reputation for selflessness and altruism. A few standout examples are Patagonia (USA), Auroville (India), The Akshaya Patra Foundation (India), Narayana Health (India), Ben &

Jerry's (USA), Sarvodaya (Sri Lanka), IKEA (Sweden) and Eileen Fisher (USA). They have shown it is possible to be both profitable and ethical; that business can be a force for good in the world, and can lead to long-term success and a positive impact on both the company and society as a whole.

Chapter Summary

- Altruism helps and complements leaders in their decision-making process by incorporating kindness, generosity, compassion and more, which in turn makes them more ethical and trustworthy.
- Altruistic leaders exemplify strong qualities such as patience, faith and perseverance, while also achieving their goals and objectives.
- Practicing altruism means aligning with nature's principle of working for the greater good, ensuring that everyone and everything receives a fair share. This abides by divine laws, which dictate that giving and receiving are interconnected.
- Altruism aligns with the principles of minimalism and lean philosophy, which have become the de facto norms for modern organizations.

The most challenging aspect of pursuing altruism and selflessness is the art of balancing an individual's self-interest with the well-being of others, transcending mere skill into an art form.

6

The Interplay of Spiritual Quotient and Organizational Growth

yaṁ hi na vyathayantyete puruṣaṁ puruṣarṣhabha
sama-duḥkha-sukhaṁ dhīraṁ so 'mṛitatvāya kalpate

(O Arjun, noblest amongst men! A person who is not affected by happiness and distress, and remains steady in the face of both, becomes eligible for liberation.)
—Bhagavad Gita, chapter 2, verse 15

Context

This shloka encapsulates the entire concept of emotional intelligence (EI). In the corporate world, where leaders navigate the ups and downs of business, maintaining poise becomes crucial. Most leaders enter with a reasonably high IQ shaped by their background and, over the years, they tend to refine their emotional quotient (EQ) by empathetically managing people.

To complete their leadership skills, they must also integrate a Spiritual Quotient (SQ), allowing them to make decisions from a heart-centred perspective. When a leader adopts such an approach, employees reciprocate by demonstrating similar behaviour as well.

Prelude

SQ refers to an individual's capacity to connect with a higher purpose or meaning in life, as well as to develop qualities such as compassion, empathy and wisdom.

Organizational growth, on the other hand, pertains to the increase in size, profitability and productivity of a business or other types of organizations.

The specific relationship between these factors will vary from one organization to another; there is no one-size-fits-all answer. However, there are general principles that can be applied to help organizations achieve growth and success.

Organizations that prioritize spiritual values like integrity, ethics and social responsibility may experience sustainable growth over the long term. Such organizations tend to build stronger relationships with customers, employees and stakeholders, translating into greater loyalty, trust and goodwill.

Leaders with a high SQ are better equipped to inspire and motivate their teams. They navigate complex situations with clarity and equanimity, and foster innovation and creativity. These qualities can lead to new products, services or business models, driving growth.

Organizational growth involves various factors, including financial resources, market conditions, and the economy. However, by focusing on leadership and the spiritual quotient, organizations can increase their chances of growth and success.

But, as mentioned above, the relationship between SQ and organizational growth is not always straightforward or predictable. Some organizations may prioritize profit at the expense of spiritual values, while others struggle to balance commercial success with meaningful work.

Ultimately, the interplay between SQ and organizational growth requires ongoing attention, reflection and dialogue. By cultivating awareness of these concepts and their interconnectedness, leaders and organizations foster a holistic and sustainable approach to growth and development.

Sahadeva, the All-Knower

Let me take you back to one of the lesser-known heroes of the Mahabharata—Sahadeva, the youngest of the five Pandavas, born to their father Pandu's second wife, Madri.

Pandu was regarded as the most knowledgeable individual of his time. In the final years before his demise, he expresses a strange desire to his sons—that he has a lot to offer, and the best way for them to gain from it will be to consume his flesh, particularly his brain, after his death. Hearing this from their father is daunting, and four of the five Pandavas don't go through with it. Sahadeva, however, meticulously follows his father's instructions after his demise, consuming three mouthfuls of flesh and brain.

The first mouthful grants him complete knowledge of the universe's past; the second of the universe's present; and the third of its future secrets, no matter how distant. Consequently, Sahadeva is armed with comprehensive knowledge of the Mahabharata war and forthcoming events over time. Generally, only a high-calibre saint or possessor of knowledge (gyaani) has the ability to perceive the past, present and future as a cohesive fabric.

This is precisely why Duryodhana approaches Sahadeva to ask for the most auspicious date to commence the war, which would ensure victory for the Kauravas. Duryodhana believes that Sahadeva's unparalleled wisdom would ensure accuracy, and has faith in his neutrality, despite belonging to the opposing side.

Nevertheless, a series of unanswered questions lingers. Why didn't Sahadeva prevent his older brother Yudhishthira from engaging in the game of dice in Hastinapur, which ultimately resulted in their exile? Why didn't Sahadeva intervene to halt the atrocities befalling his own brothers? Why didn't he avert the downfall of his own blood relatives and cousins on the opposing side? He possessed foreknowledge of all impending events, and yet he didn't leverage this knowledge for the advantage of his family. Does this knowledge have any value when it's not utilized to benefit one's own family? Was Sahadeva justified in his silence?

When examined closely, you will find he was bound by an oath similar to Bhishma's—an oath to withhold the truth. Yet, no one had explicitly told him: 'Do not share what you know.' For whatever reason—karma, fate, the divine play of Lord Krishna—Sahadeva chose silence.

Another intriguing aspect is that Sahadeva was the only Pandava who boldly expressed his disapproval to Lord Krishna. As per author's inference from his knowledge of the Mahabharata, in Krishna's plan, even the Pandavas were intended to be killed in the war. Sahadeva saw through to the end, and affectionately warned him: 'If you proceed, I will bind you in my heart with my love, and prevent you from executing this war.' Krishna confessed to the plan, saying: 'Sahadeva, please refrain from this, or my designs will be thwarted.' Ultimately, a resolution was reached, with Lord Krishna permitting the Pandavas, Draupadi, and one of their offspring to survive. This marked the conclusion of the war.

But why did Sahadev remain silent other than at this one instance? He had known of the impending war from a young age. Yet, he chose not to alter the course of events, and refrained from influencing the outcomes. He could have easily shared his foreknowledge, fostering amicable settlements among his brothers, cousins and other relatives.

The key questions this story raises are: Does dharma lie in possessing complete knowledge of the past, present and future, and yet remaining silent? Is there any dharma in allowing one's cousins to perish when one holds the power to potentially change the entire course of the Mahabharata? Was Sahadeva's silence solely governed by Lord Krishna's decree or did he possess the freedom to make his own choices? After all, if Lord Krishna was there to restore dharma, wasn't it Sahadeva's responsibility to influence him and ensure peaceful coexistence between the Pandavas and the Kauravas?[1]

What are the dharmic dynamics at play here? Do you encounter individuals who possess the truth, who are aware of what lies ahead, who in their hearts could differentiate right from wrong, and yet choose silence, allowing others to endure life's upheavals, changes and challenges? Was Sahadeva right or wrong in his silence? What parallels do you see in your own life, where individuals play similar roles?

Let us contemplate the shifting dharmic equations, affected by Sahadeva's action or inaction; discern what we can learn from this tale for our own lives; consider how we can stand up for the truth, and when necessary, employ truth itself to make dharma more palatable to those around us, without being passive bystanders.

There is another story I'd like to share, again from the Mahabharata, to drive home the link between SQ and organizational growth.

Raja Dharma and the Spiritual Quotient

During the time of the Mahabharata, there is a wise king named Raja Dharma, renowned for his righteousness, compassion and profound spiritual understanding. He rules over a prosperous kingdom, where people live in harmony, and flourish.

One day, Raja Dharma decides to assess the spiritual quotient of his subjects, for gauging their inner well-being. He disguises himself as a commoner and traverses his kingdom, engaging with people from all walks of life.

He encounters a destitute farmer who struggles to make ends meet, but despite his hardships, greets the disguised king with a smile, offers him food and shelter. The farmer's selflessness and kindness deeply touch the king, prompting him to inquire about the source of the farmer's happiness.

'Noble sir, my happiness emanates from contentment and gratitude. Although I lack material wealth, I'm thankful for what I have, and find joy in aiding others. My faith in the divine and my connection with nature keep me grounded and serene,' the farmer says.

Impressed by the farmer's elevated SQ, Raja Dharma continues his journey, and encounters a wealthy merchant known for his greed and deceit. The merchant amasses wealth and exploits the poor for personal gains. The disguised king confronts the merchant, seeking to understand his actions.

Caught off-guard, the merchant attempts to justify his behaviour by asserting that wealth is the key to happiness and power. He believes that material possessions and worldly success define a person's worth. Raja Dharma realizes that the merchant's low SQ exacerbates societal harm, contributing to inequality and unrest.

Raja Dharma then reveals his true identity to the merchant and expounds on the significance of spiritual quotient in state progress. He shares that genuine wealth and success spring from cultivating virtues such as compassion, honesty and selflessness. He explains that a high SQ fosters a society where people unite, harmonize and collaborate for the greater good.

Touched by Raja Dharma's words, the merchant recognizes his error and pledges to change. He begins using his wealth for the welfare of the people, inspiring others to follow suit. The merchant's transformation catalyses a positive shift in the overall well-being of the kingdom's citizens.

Raja Dharma's emphasis on spiritual quotient as a governing principle for both leadership and personal development propels his kingdom's growth. His sagacious and compassionate leadership becomes an exemplar for other rulers, and his realm evolves into a symbol of prosperity and harmony. As time passes, his legacy of valuing spiritual quotient spreads far and wide, becoming a guiding principle not only for his kingdom, but also for neighboring realms.

The tale of Raja Dharma's judicious rule, and his emphasis on spiritual quotient, evolved into a legend passed down through generations, reminding people of the significance of inner well-being for the advancement of a state.

How the Tale Connects to the Corporate World

The concept of SQ extends beyond solely spiritual pursuits; it pertains to an individual's level of spiritual intelligence, encompassing the capacity to comprehend and navigate the deeper meanings and purpose of life, establish profound connections with others, possess self-awareness, and embrace an interconnectedness with the world around us, even including the ability to glimpse into the future!

The SQ encompasses a diverse array of qualities, such as empathy, compassion, gratitude, and the capability to uncover significance and purpose in life. It entails recognizing and appreciating the interdependence of all things, and comprehending the role each individual plays in the grander scheme.

Fundamentally, SQ involves nurturing a sense of internal wisdom, and a connection to something greater than oneself, then leveraging this awareness to make constructive contributions to the world. This process might involve spiritual practices, but it can also encompass the development of other facets of our emotional, social and intellectual intelligence.

In sum, SQ represents a comprehensive approach to personal growth and development, encompassing all dimensions of our existence: mind, body and spirit.

Both these aforementioned tales have a profound affinity with SQ. Sahadeva's capacity to forge a deep connection to the past, present and future through the gifts bestowed upon him by his father not only aids him, but also secures the reign of the Pandavas into the future. Similarly, a CEO might need to seek inner guidance about the future, and how to lead their company through challenging periods, sometimes even at the expense of competitors. It's a paradoxical notion, yet one that warrants contemplation.

Similarly, Raja Dharma's SQ-driven approach to governance serves as a model worth emulating in today's corporate realm.

Questions that Matter

How can spirituality contribute to an individual's IQ and EQ?

It can contribute significantly by fostering holistic personal development.

Regarding IQ, spiritual practices like meditation and yoga enhance cognitive functions. Regular practice improves attention, memory and problem-solving abilities, elevating intellectual capacity.

The contemplative nature of spirituality encourages critical thinking, self-awareness and open-mindedness, which all contribute to higher cognitive functioning.

In terms of EQ, spirituality plays a pivotal role in emotional intelligence. With increased self-awareness and regulation, one is more likely to respond thoughtfully rather than reactively in interpersonal interactions. Additionally, a strong sense of purpose and connectedness to something larger than oneself can reduce stress and increase one's capacity to manage emotional challenges.

What is SQ and how can it be used to measure an individual's spiritual awareness and growth?

An individual's SQ is a measure of their level of spiritual awareness and growth. It is based on the idea that spirituality is a distinct aspect of intelligence, separate from IQ and EQ, and can be quantified using a specific set of criteria.

The concept of SQ was first introduced by psychologist Danah Zohar in her 2000 book *SQ: Spiritual Intelligence, The Ultimate Intelligence*. According to Zohar, SQ includes four key components:

Self-awareness: The ability to reflect on one's own thoughts, feelings, and beliefs, to understand how they influence one's actions and interactions with others.

Compassion: The ability to feel empathy and compassion for others, and to act in a way that promotes the well-being of all.

Inner life: The ability to connect with one's inner self, through practices such as meditation, prayer or contemplation, and to find meaning and purpose in life.

Vision and values: The ability to have a clear vision of one's own values and goals, and to align one's actions with these values in a way that contributes to the greater good.

To measure an individual's SQ, various tools and assessments have been developed to evaluate these four components. These assessments may include self-reporting questionnaires, interviews or observational measures.

The idea of SQ is still evolving, and there is an ongoing debate about whether spirituality can be accurately measured in this way. However, proponents of SQ argue that it can be a useful tool for assessing an individual's spiritual growth and development, and for identifying areas for further personal and spiritual development.

How can spirituality help individuals develop an adaptability quotient (AQ), and improve their ability to adapt to change?

This refers to an individual's ability to adapt to change, whether it be in their personal or professional life. Spirituality can help individuals develop an AQ by providing them with the necessary tools and mindset to navigate uncertainty and change. Spirituality helps by fostering qualities and perspectives that enhance their ability to navigate change effectively.

Here are some specific examples of how spirituality can help individuals be adaptive to change:
- A person who is facing job loss may find comfort in their spiritual beliefs, which can help them to see the situation as an opportunity to find a new job that is a better fit for them.

- A person who is going through a divorce may find strength in their spiritual community, which can help them to cope with the emotional challenges of the situation.
- A person who is moving to a new city may find comfort in their spiritual practices, which can help them to feel connected to some semblance of familiarity in a new and unfamiliar environment.

By integrating these spiritual principles and practices into their lives, individuals can enhance their AQ. This, in turn, equips them with the mental, emotional and interpersonal tools needed to navigate change, seize opportunities, and thrive in an ever-evolving world. No matter what challenges we face in life, spirituality can help us to adapt to change and to find meaning in the midst of it all.

How can a company foster a culture that promotes the development of employees' IQ, EQ, SQ and AQ?

Fostering a culture that promotes the holistic development these quotients requires a comprehensive and intentional approach:

Learning and development programmes: Offer a range of training and skill-building programmes that enhance employees' cognitive abilities, emotional intelligence, spiritual awareness and adaptability. These should cater to various learning styles and preferences.

Wellness initiatives: Integrate heartfulness/mindfulness practices, meditation sessions and wellness programmes to cultivate emotional resilience, self-awareness and spiritual growth among employees. Such initiatives create a balanced and focused workforce.

Value-based leadership: Encourage leaders to model values aligned with IQ, EQ, SQ and AQ. Leaders who prioritize ethical decision-making, empathy, open communication and adaptability set a powerful example for employees to follow.

Feedback and self-reflection: Instil a culture of continuous feedback and self-reflection. Encourage employees to assess their own growth in terms of intelligence, emotional awareness, spiritual alignment and adaptability.

Flexible work environment: Provide flexibility in work arrangements, recognizing the importance of work-life balance and adaptability in navigating changing circumstances.

Inclusive communication: Foster open communication that respects diverse viewpoints and encourages EQ. Regular discussions about personal growth, well-being and adaptability normalize these aspects within the company culture.

Emphasize adaptability: Encouraging employees to embrace change and develop their AQ can help them be more resilient and adaptable in the face of uncertainty. This can be done by providing opportunities for employees to work on projects outside of their comfort zones, or by encouraging them to seek out new experiences.

Recognition and rewards: Recognize employees who exhibit growth in IQ, EQ, SQ, and AQ. Tie recognition and rewards to these developmental dimensions to reinforce their importance.

Leadership development: Invest in leadership development programmes that emphasize the importance of emotional intelligence, adaptability and spiritual values in effective leadership.

Clear values and mission: Define the company's values and mission in a way that encompasses IQ, EQ, SQ and AQ. Employees should understand how their personal development aligns with the organization's overall purpose.

By nurturing a culture that recognizes the interconnectedness of IQ, EQ, SQ, and AQ, companies empower employees to thrive intellectually, emotionally, spiritually and adaptively. This holistic approach not only enhances individual growth but also contributes to a collaborative, resilient and purpose-driven organizational culture, and ultimately, a more successful organization.

What are some real-life examples of Indian and Asian organizations that have successfully integrated spirituality into their employees' personal and professional development, leading to improved performance and business outcomes?

There are several Indian and Asian companies that have accomplished this:

Bharat Petroleum Corporation Limited: This Indian state-owned oil and gas company has a spirituality and wellness programme that is designed to help employees manage stress, improve their overall health, and connect with their inner selves. The programme offers a variety of activities, including yoga, meditation, and spiritual talks. The company has also been recognized for its commitment to social responsibility, winning numerous awards for its corporate citizenship initiatives.

Azim Premji Foundation: This Indian non-profit founded by Wipro chair Azim Premji, is on a mission to improve the quality of life of the underprivileged in India. The foundation has a number of programmes and initiatives that focus on education, health and livelihood. The foundation has also been recognized for its commitment to social responsibility, winning numerous awards for its corporate citizenship initiatives.

Sri Aurobindo Ashram: This spiritual community in Puducherry was founded by Sri Aurobindo, a philosopher and yogi. The ashram offers a variety of programmes and initiatives that focus on spirituality, yoga and meditation. The ashram has also been recognized for its commitment to social responsibility, winning numerous awards for its humanitarian work.

Isha Foundation: This non-profit organization, founded by yogi and mystic Sadhguru Jaggi Vasudev, offers a variety of programmes and initiatives that focus on spirituality, yoga and meditation. The foundation has also been recognized for its commitment to social responsibility, winning numerous awards for its humanitarian work.

Infosys: This Indian multinational IT company has a long history of integrating spirituality into its culture. Infosys offers a number of programmes and initiatives to support the spiritual development of its employees, including yoga classes, meditation sessions and spiritual retreats. The company has also been recognized for its commitment to social responsibility and its corporate citizenship initiatives.

Mahindra Group: This group emphasizes the principles of 'Rise for Good', promoting sustainability, community development and ethical behaviour. These values reflect spiritual principles, and contribute to both business growth and societal progress.

The Heartfulness Institute: While specific business outcomes may not be directly applicable as the organization is more focused on individual growth, there are several ways in which the Heartfulness

Institute has successfully integrated spirituality into the well-being and growth of its members, which can indirectly influence their performance and contribute to positive outcomes. It includes Stress Reduction, Enhanced Emotional Intelligence, Resilience, Work-life Balance, Clarity of Thought and Improved mental, emotional and physical well-being.

Chapter Summary

- Cultivating a higher Spiritual Quotient (SQ) can lead to the taming of other quotients such as IQ, EQ and beyond, with comparatively less effort over time.
- SQ, representing an individual's capacity to connect with a higher purpose or meaning in life, can be seen as an attempt to establish a connection with the natural world.
- SQ's growth is directly proportional to individual growth, and as a leader nurtures it, it significantly impacts organizational growth.
- The balance between SQ and organizational growth mirrors the implementation of corporate social responsibility, and serves as an indicator of sustainable growth.

Leaders with high SQ should aim to contribute not only to organizational growth, but also to the broader socio-economic and regional growth, reflecting a holistic approach to leadership.

7

Humility and a Sense of Groundedness

vidyā-vinaya-sampanne brāhmaṇe gavi hastini śhuni chaiva śhva-pāke cha paṇḍitāḥ sama-darśhinaḥ

(The truly learned, with the eyes of divine knowledge, see a Brahmin, a cow, an elephant, a dog, and a dog-eater with equanimity.)

—Bhagavad Gita, chapter 5, verse 18

Context

The true indicator of divine knowledge is humility, while shallow, bookish knowledge tends to foster the pride of scholarship.

In the long run, employees tend to follow leaders who embody humility and remain grounded. Arrogant leaders might achieve short-term results through a forceful approach, but people are more inclined to work for leaders who demonstrate empathy and skilfully persuade others, with humility, to fulfil their commitments. Developing humility can be a challenge for leaders accustomed to a Type A personality, yet this trait becomes indispensable as leaders expand their scope.

Prelude

Humility and groundedness are indispensable qualities for effective leaders. These attributes enable leaders to connect with their team members, cultivate trust, and establish a collaborative and positive work atmosphere.

Leaders who embody these qualities recognize that they do not possess all the answers, and are willing to listen to others' viewpoints and ideas. They maintain an open-minded and approachable demeanour, making it more conducive for team members to communicate with them. This, in turn, facilitates enhanced problem-solving and decision-making.

Leaders who exhibit humility and groundedness are less likely to allow their egos to hinder rational decision-making. They readily acknowledge their errors and take ownership of their mistakes. This behaviour contributes to nurturing a culture of responsibility and ownership among team members.

Furthermore, leaders who exemplify humility and groundedness demonstrate greater empathy and compassion towards their team members. They acknowledge that every individual possesses strengths and weaknesses, and they actively work towards fostering an inclusive environment where everyone feels valued and acknowledged.

High-level leaders who embrace the qualities being highlighted in this chapter are more accessible and receptive. This enables them to establish connections with their team members, grasp their concerns, and foster trust. Consequently, team members are more inclined to express their thoughts, feedback and challenges to the leader, ultimately resulting in improved decision-making and problem-solving.

Arjuna's Pride

The twists and turns that greet even the greatest of warriors in a story like the Mahabharata could lead one to conclude how stupid humans are; how we refuse to understand divine intervention and the support in the work that we do.

Even a person of the calibre of Arjuna, the hero of the Mahabharata, doesn't yet understand that he is almost nothing without the support of Lord Krishna.

On the seventeenth day of the war, when Karna is leading the Kaurava army (and will go on to finally fall), he and Arjuna are locked in intense battle. Several times, Arjuna, the skilled warrior, is able to push Karna's chariot back by almost ten hastas (ten feet) each. Yet, Karna fights on, and manages to push his chariot forward and Arjuna's chariot (being piloted by Lord Krishna) back by about two feet each time.

Arjuna is immensely proud of this difference in the distances the chariots are being pushed back.

On one of his attempts to come forward again, Karna's chariot gets stuck in the mud, owing to a curse he had incurred. This is when Arjuna finishes him off, at the behest of Lord Krishna. Arjuna actually wants to wait, because it is not fair to kill a person who is not in a position to fight back, but Krishna reminds him of his duty.

Once Karna's soul leaves his body, Lord Krishna keeps heaping praise on his ability in battle, and what a great fight he had given to Arjuna. This makes Arjuna upset, and he keeps asking why the Lord keeps praising Karna, when it was he who was pushing the latter's chariot much further back. Lord Krishna simply smiles, but doesn't say anything on that day.

The next day turns out to be the final day of the war—Duryodhana falls, and the conch is blown to technically end the war, despite Ashwathama having other plans.

Now, Arjuna tells Lord Krishna that owing to his respect for him, he will only get out of the chariot once the Lord has done so. But Krishna repeatedly tells him to get down first. Arjuna keeps insisting. 'No, no, you have to get down first, because I am the one who is inside the chariot, and you are the one who is driving me.' But Krishna also insists that Arjuna get down first, and the latter eventually obeys.

Once Krishna follows Arjuna out of the chariot, the flag of Lord Hanuman, which was on the top of the chariot, disappears into thin air. Then, Lord Krishna takes the horses pulling the chariot to safety. Immediately, the chariot goes up in flames, leaving Arjuna dumbstruck—how could this happen to the special chariot gifted to him by Agni, the god of fire, himself?

The backstory of the chariot is as follows: one day, when Lord Agni was very hungry, he wanted to devour a forest called the Khandava forest. But he was stopped by Indra, the rain god and king of the gods, because a friend of his, a serpent king, resided in the forest. With the help of the water god, Varuna, Indra keeps pouring rain and dousing the flames of Agni, thus denying him food. At this time, Arjuna comes to the aid of Agni, fights against his own biological father (Indra) and defeats him, allowing Agni to devour the forest and satiate his hunger. Agni is so happy with Arjuna that he gifts him this chariot, and says: 'This has such a shield of protection that nothing can happen to it.' Agni also gave him four splendid horses to pull the chariot.

Now, Lord Krishna answers Arjuna's question from the previous day: 'You said you were a better fighter than Karna because your chariot was being pushed back only by two feet. The person on the other side had no protection whatsoever, was already disarmed, and also carried curses, like the one that ensured his chariot was stuck in the mud. Despite that, he was able to push your chariot back by two feet—a chariot given to you by Lord Agni, protected by the flag of Lord Hanuman; you also had me, the Lord of the universe, with you. With all this, Karna was still able to push you back. What kind of a warrior must he have been?'

Arjuna bows his head, finally understanding that Karna was a far superior warrior, and but for Lord Krishna's protection, he would not have been able to accomplish what he did.

Then, the second question comes up—why did the chariot go up in flames? Lord Krishna says with a smile: 'From day one, you were attacked by the best warriors from the other side, such as Bhishma, Dronacharya, Kripacharya, Karna—you name one, and they would have all attacked you in one form or another. They were all using divine astras. All of them were neutralized because I was there, and also due to the power of the chariot. Lord Agni himself was giving you a protective shield. The moment the war was over, those protective shields were removed. Had I got down first and allowed you to get down later, you and the horses would have gone up in flames.'

Arjuna then falls at the Lord's feet, crying. 'What a mistake I have made! I have been repeatedly underestimating the role that you have been playing. And despite that, you have always been with me and supported me.'

Lord Krishna accepts his humility with a big smile, and gives him a hug.

How the Tale Connects to the Corporate World

Think how various divine powers came together to assist Arjuna, all to safeguard dharma. Similarly, in our own lives, we often fail to recognize the contributions of gods, gurus, coaches, mentors and our teams. Instead, we tend to attribute even minor successes solely to ourselves, disregarding the fact that we are mere pawns in a grander scheme, where the ultimate goal is always the restoration of dharma. Whenever entropy sets in, leading to regression, these exceptional personalities emerge to offer their guidance and support. This is exactly what Lord Krishna says in the Gita in the famous shloka:

'Yadā yadā hi dharmasya glānir bhavati bhārata
abhyutthānam adharmasya tadātmānaṁ sṛijāmyaham'

While we have the ability to regulate our efforts, actions and attitudes towards a given situation, we are not always in control of the final outcome or results. External factors frequently come into play, influencing the consequences of our actions. These factors could include the actions of others, unforeseen events or circumstances.

For instance, an athlete can manage their training regimen, nutritional intake and mental outlook towards their sport, but they cannot dictate the weather, the performance of their competitors or any potential injuries that might arise during a competition.

Likewise, in the professional realm, an employee can control their productivity, communication, and work ethic, but they may not always have sway over the decisions made by their superiors, the conduct of their colleagues, or changes in the market or industry.

Nevertheless, it is crucial to recognize that even though we may not have complete command over the results, our influence on them can be substantial—by concentrating on the factors within our control. Exerting our utmost effort and adopting a proactive approach to resolving challenges can enhance the likelihood of achieving the desired outcome.

In essence, while we may lack complete authority over the results, we do possess power over our endeavours and perspectives concerning a situation; factors that can profoundly impact the final outcome.

If you take Lord Krishna to be Arjuna's coach, a few things shall fall into proper perspective.

Coaches and mentors play a pivotal role in assisting and guiding us through situations that may appear to be beyond our control. Their wealth of expertise, experience and support can be incredibly valuable in such circumstances. They offer a fresh perspective, provide objective feedback, and aid in the development of strategies and skills necessary to surmount challenges and attain our objectives.

A key way in which coaches and mentors assist us is by creating a safe and nurturing environment for discussing our concerns, fears and aspirations. Through active listening and thought-provoking inquiries, they help us attain clarity and insight into our situation, enabling us to identify potential solutions and courses of action.

Moreover, coaches and mentors are valuable sources of guidance and advice, drawing from their personal experiences and expertise. They readily share their knowledge, impart practical tips and strategies, and contribute to the enhancement of our competencies and strengths.

In addition, coaches and mentors provide motivation and encouragement, aiding us in maintaining focus on our goals. They hold us accountable, offer unwavering support, and share in celebrating our achievements throughout our journey.

These mentors help cultivate our resilience and coping skills to navigate challenging circumstances. Through modelling positive behaviours and attitudes, providing emotional backing and assisting in reframing our perspective, they empower us to manage stress and uncertainty, and develop the confidence and resilience essential for overcoming obstacles and realizing our aspirations.

Questions that Matter

How can spirituality help individuals develop a sense of humility and groundedness in a corporate setting?

Spirituality can play a transformative role in nurturing humility and groundedness. In the fast-paced, competitive and often ego-driven world of business, incorporating spiritual principles can help employees and leaders reconnect with their authentic selves and cultivate a more balanced perspective.

Spirituality encourages individuals to recognize their interconnectedness with others and the world around them. By embracing the idea that all beings are part of a larger whole, individuals develop a sense of humility that acknowledges their place within a vast web of relationships. This perspective naturally humbles the ego, as it shifts the focus from self-centered achievements to a collective purpose. By understanding that success is interconnected and shared, individuals become less driven by the need for personal recognition, and more by the desire to contribute meaningfully to the greater good of the organization and society.

Spiritual practices, such as meditation and introspection, create a space for self-reflection. Regular introspection enables individuals to identify and acknowledge their strengths and weaknesses, fostering a genuine and grounded self-awareness. This becomes a foundation for humility, as individuals recognize that they are continuously learning and evolving. By acknowledging their imperfections, employees and leaders become more approachable and open to collaboration, creating a harmonious corporate environment.

In a world of constant change and uncertainty, spirituality also teaches individuals the value of embracing impermanence. Recognizing that situations are transient, and that no one has complete control over outcomes, humbles the desire for power and control. This acceptance of impermanence encourages adaptability and flexibility, enabling individuals to navigate challenges with grace and resilience.

Here are some examples of how this can all work out in a corporate setting:

A salesperson who is constantly striving to close deals may find that spirituality helps them to step back and see the bigger picture. They may realize that their work is not just about making money, but also about helping people. This can help them to develop a sense of humility and compassion with their customers.

A manager who is constantly stressed out about meeting deadlines may find that spirituality helps them relax and focus on the present moment. They may realize they cannot control everything, and that it is important to let go of some of their stress. This can help them develop a sense of groundedness, and be more effective at work.

An employee who is feeling burnt out may find that spirituality helps them to connect with their inner selves and to find meaning in their work. They may realize that their work is not just about a paycheck, but also about making a difference in the world. This can help them develop a sense of humility and be more motivated at work.

Spirituality offers invaluable tools by emphasizing interconnectedness, self-awareness, values-based living and empathy. In this way, individuals are prompted to transcend ego-driven pursuits and embrace a more balanced and meaningful approach to their roles. As employees and leaders embody these qualities, they contribute to an organizational culture that prioritizes collaboration, shared purpose, and genuine care for one another. Thus, spirituality fosters an environment where humility and groundedness thrive, leading to improved employee well-being, teamwork and, ultimately, enhanced business outcomes.

What spiritual principles or practices can be used to cultivate a sense of humility and groundedness among employees?

Several practices rooted in spirituality can effectively foster these qualities.

Meditation: This can help us focus our attention on the present, and let go of distractions, which develops a sense of humility, as we realize that our 'self' is not just our thoughts or emotions. It can also help us to feel more grounded, as we connect with our inner selves and with the present.

Yoga: This combines physical postures, breathing exercises and meditation. It can help us to improve our flexibility, strength and balance, and develop a sense of humility, as we learn to accept our bodies and limitations. It can also help us feel more grounded, as we connect with our breath and our bodies.

Prayer: This is a practice of communication with a higher power, which can help connect with something bigger than ourselves, and find meaning in our lives. It can also help us to develop a sense of humility, as we realize that we are not in control of everything.

Open-mindedness: Spiritual practices often emphasize the value of being open to new ideas and perspectives. Encouraging employees to actively listen to colleagues, seek feedback and consider viewpoints different from their own cultivates humility, by acknowledging that one's perspective is just one of many valid viewpoints.

Leadership by example: Leaders should embody the spiritual principles they want to cultivate among employees. When leaders demonstrate humility, transparency and open-mindedness, employees are more likely to follow suit. Authentic leadership creates an atmosphere where humility is valued and practiced.

How can a company promote a culture of humility and groundedness while also achieving business objectives?

Promoting such a culture in a corporate setting can be beneficial not only for the well-being of employees, but also for the achievement of business objectives. Here are some ways to do that.

Recognize and celebrate successes: Celebrating achievements is important, as is recognizing the contributions of all team members. Creating a culture that recognizes the value of each individual's contributions, no matter how small, can help foster humility and groundedness.

Encourage diversity and inclusion: A diverse and inclusive work environment can help foster humility and groundedness by recognizing the value of different perspectives and experiences.

Provide opportunities for personal and professional development: This can help employees develop a greater sense of self-awareness and humility. Steps can include mentoring, coaching and training programmes.

How can spirituality help leaders and managers stay grounded and maintain perspective in high-pressure situations?

First, practices such as meditation and self-reflection cultivate a calm and centred mind. These techniques enable leaders to detach from the chaos of the moment, fostering mental clarity and preventing impulsive decisions driven by stress.

Second, spiritual principles emphasize humility and interconnectedness. When leaders acknowledge their role as part of a larger whole, their ego-driven desires for control and recognition diminish. This perspective helps leaders focus on collective success rather than the personal, leading to more balanced decision-making.

Here are some examples:

- A CEO facing a financial crisis may find that spirituality helps them stay calm and focused. They may realize that the crisis is not the end of the world, and that they can get through it. This can help them make sound decisions and lead their company through the crisis.
- A manager dealing with a difficult employee may find that spirituality helps them be more compassionate. They may realize that employees are struggling with their own issues, and

need understanding. This can help resolve the situation in a positive way.
- An employee feeling stressed out may find that spirituality helps them find meaning in their work. They may realize that their work is not just about a paycheck, but also about making a difference in the world. This can help them stay motivated and do their best work.

Humility and groundedness appear to me more as 'lame duck' stuff. Is it truly worth following on the personal, professional and business fronts?

At a glance, these may seem like vague and unassertive qualities in a world driven by competition and ambition. However, upon closer examination, humility and groundedness hold immense value on the personal, professional and business fronts, offering individuals and organizations substantial benefits that far outweigh any misconceived notions of weakness.

On a personal level, these qualities foster genuine self-awareness. Recognizing one's limitations and imperfections forms the foundation for growth and learning. Embracing humility encourages openness to feedback and the willingness to acknowledge mistakes, leading to continuous self-improvement. Groundedness ensures that individuals maintain a balanced perspective, preventing the lure of ego-driven pursuits that can lead to burnout or disillusionment. These qualities create a stronger sense of authenticity and integrity, enabling individuals to form deeper and more meaningful connections with others.

In the professional realm, these are assets that fuel effective leadership. Leaders who exhibit these qualities are more approachable and relatable to their teams, fostering a culture of open communication and trust. Humble leaders prioritize collective success over personal recognition, fostering collaboration and shared achievements. Grounded leaders maintain composure under pressure, making well-informed decisions based on a clear and rational assessment of situations. This cultivates a resilient and adaptive work environment that is better equipped to navigate challenges.

If you are looking to improve your life, I encourage you to cultivate humility and groundedness; they are essential for success in all areas of life.

Chapter Summary

- Humility signifies an open heart and mind, demonstrating the individual's willingness to listen to others.
- To be humble means embracing one's present state without artifice or hypocrisy—neither more nor less. When leaders cultivate this quality, it signals their approachability and trustworthiness.
- It serves as a protective layer or shield during times of both success and adversity. Leaders who nurture this quality can steer their organizations resolutely, regardless of the circumstances.
- It also signifies recognizing that an individual's knowledge is minuscule compared to the entirety of existence, fostering a willingness to learn continuously. As the wise often emphasize, 'learning never stops'.
- However, being humble does not equate to perpetually tolerating others' errors or mistakes. Instead, it implies recognizing that beyond certain limits, it becomes necessary to take appropriate measures and courageous steps to address and guide others in rectifying such situations.

8

Guided by a Larger Purpose/ Cause—The Unsolved Mysteries

karmaṇy-evādhikāras te mā phaleṣhu kadāchana mā karma-phala-hetur bhūr mā te saṅgo 'stvakarmaṇi

(You have a right to perform your prescribed duties, but you are not entitled to the fruits of your actions. Never consider yourself to be the cause of the results of your activities, nor be attached to inaction.)

—Bhagavad Gita, chapter 2, verse 47

Context

Often, a lack of clarity makes leaders settle for smaller dreams. As the Gita says, we are kept from our goal not by obstacles, but by a clear path to a lesser goal, or a smaller sense of purpose or lack thereof. As a leader, one might be tempted sometimes to take the easier path, but this shloka reminds us to be committed to our work and aim for a higher goal. At the same time, as one starts ascending greater heights, it is harmful to become feverish about results, as one may lose balance quickly. In other words, stick to the path, and learn to cherish the journey more than the destination.

Prelude

Guided by a larger purpose or cause, solving mysteries that continue to elude explanation can be a compelling and meaningful endeavour. Countless such mysteries exist across the world, ranging from the origins of the universe to the disappearances of individuals, groups or lifeforms.

One benefit of such a pursuit is the potential to unlock knowledge and understanding about the world and our place in it. For example, searching for answers about the formation of the universe has led to significant advancements in astrophysics and cosmology.

Solving such mysteries can bring closure and justice to those affected by them. For instance, discovering new evidence in a cold case can provide closure to the families of victims, or aid in exonerating someone who was wrongly accused.

Solving these mysteries can also foster a sense of curiosity and wonder, inspiring individuals to think creatively and critically. By encouraging people to question assumptions and explore new ideas, the process can lead to personal growth and intellectual development.

Ultimately, the pursuit can serve as a unifying force, bringing together individuals with diverse backgrounds and expertise to work towards a common goal. Whether driven by curiosity, justice or a desire to advance knowledge, solving mysteries can be a powerful and rewarding experience.

Unsolved mysteries can have a paradoxical impact on leadership—both as a source of inspiration, and as a potential distraction or hindrance.

They can inspire leaders to think outside the box, challenge assumptions and pursue innovative solutions. By engaging with complex and difficult questions, leaders can sharpen their critical thinking and problem-solving skills, inspiring their teams to do the same. Additionally, the pursuit can be a powerful motivator, driving individuals to push beyond their limits and pursue ambitious goals.

On the other hand, unsolved mysteries can also be a distraction, pushing leaders and their teams to focus on questions that may never be fully answered. In some cases, leaders may become so consumed with the pursuit that they neglect other important tasks or priorities. This can be particularly problematic when pressing issues require immediate attention, or when the resources devoted to solving a mystery could be better utilized elsewhere.

Furthermore, this pursuit can create uncertainty and ambiguity that can be challenging for leaders. When no clear answer or solution is in sight, leaders may struggle to make informed decisions or communicate effectively with their teams. This can lead to frustration, anxiety and a lack of trust among team members.

Ultimately, the impact of unsolved mysteries on leadership will depend on how leaders approach them. By balancing curiosity and creativity with practicality and focus, leaders can harness their power to inspire and motivate their teams, while staying grounded in their mission and objectives.

We return to the Mahabharata, a treasure trove of knowledge and wisdom on dharma, swadharma and leadership. This time, we look at Duryodhana, and first acknowledge that whether he was right or wrong, he fought the war from the front.

Duryodhana's Death and His Three Questions

As the day of Duryodhana's death and the war's conclusion approaches, the battle intensifies. Finally, on Lord Krishna's advice, Bhima is able to kill his cousin. What a tragic tale! Brothers and cousins fighting—one side for dharma, and one for adharma, rooted in ego.

Even after Bhima's final blow, people are confused because Duryodhana just doesn't seem to give up life. Lord Krishna is watching from Arjuna's chariot, and Duryodhana seems to raise three fingers in the air. He is trying to communicate, but because of his near-fatal injuries, he's not able to speak.

Many warriors on the Kaurava side go near Duryodhana to see if they can understand what he wants to say, but no one does. At this moment, Krishna says 'let me communicate with him', and being the Lord himself, he dives deep into Duryodhana's consciousness and finds out what is actually stopping the soul from leaving his body. There, Krishna finds three questions Duryodhana wants answered before he dies.

One, what would Pandavas have done had Duryodhana fortified Hastinapur?

Two, when Dronacharya fell, why did Duryodhana choose Karna to lead the Kaurava force instead of Ashwathama, who was in a fit of rage because his father had been killed wrongly, and might have tilted the war in favour of the Kauravas?

The third is something many of us may not be aware of—that the strongest warrior on the Kaurava side did not fight. Vidura, half-brother to Dhritarashtra and Pandu, and prime minister of the Kuru kingdom, is said to have been such a wizard in fights that, had he participated in the war, a Kaurava victory would have been a foregone conclusion. But Vidura decided not to fight. So, Duryodhana's question to Lord Krishna was, what would've happened if he had somehow brought Vidura to the war?

Lord Krishna responds to his first question: 'Had you fortified Hastinapur, I would have made Nakula lead the Pandavas, because he has such horse-riding skill that he's even capable of riding in heavy rain without him or the horse getting wet. He has a unique ability to ride a horse even between two droplets of water, and so, would have easily entered the fort and destroyed it, defeating the Kauravas.'

For the second question, about Ashwathama, Lord Krishna says: 'It is true that if he had been made the chief in place of Karna, he might've taken the war to a different level altogether. In that case, the only way in which I would have made the Pandavas defeat the Kauravas was to make Yudhishthira (the personification of dharma, and often known as Dharma) extremely angry.'

Duryodhana is baffled, so Krishna explains: 'You're not aware of the power of Dharma. He is so calm that he has never once got angry in his life. But he also has this power that if someone really makes him angry, whatever is visible in his vicinity will be burnt down instantly, irrespective of calibre. This is a hidden power that not even Dharma is aware of, but I am aware of it. If you had brought Ashwathama to the fore, knowing that Pandavas may not be able to defeat him, I would have unleashed the hidden anger of Dharma, and all the Kauravas would've burnt down in no time. I didn't use it because there was no need.'

About the question on Vidura joining the war, Krishna says: 'Had you made Vidura fight—and he had accepted to be neutral, as

I was—I would have personally got into the battle, because the only person who can defeat Vidura is me, and no one else.'

Finally, with all the answers given, Duryodhana is satisfied, and his soul leaves the body.

There are many interesting questions to ponder in this story. If Nakula was indeed so skilled, why did Lord Krishna not make him the chief of the Pandava army? If winning the war was the goal, then why didn't Krishna make Yudhishthira angry on day one? He could've mentioned anything the Pandavas had to endure—right from the disrespect shown to Yudhishthira, the loss in the game of dice, the disrobing of Draupadi, and after they returned from their exile, the Kaurava refusal to hand over the kingdom due to them—but he didn't, so why was that? Why did Vidura, the king's brother and prime minister, choose to remain neutral? Most importantly, how can a person hold back his soul from departing his body before he receives certain answers?

How the Tale Connects to the Corporate World

Like Duryodhana's three questions, CEOs will also come across several situations and questions they need to keep finding the answers to, in order for the future of the organization to be positive.

The power of unsolved questions and mysteries in running an organization extends far beyond the conventional pursuit of clear-cut answers. While businesses often prioritize efficiency and certainty, embracing the enigmatic aspects can foster innovation, stimulate critical thinking and drive continuous improvement. These unresolved questions, often viewed as challenges, can serve as catalysts for growth and transformation, reshaping the way organizations operate and perceive their environment.

- Unanswered questions invite curiosity and exploration. In an era of rapid change, organizations that actively engage with the unknown end up cultivating a culture of curiosity. Encouraging employees to ask questions and seek solutions fosters a dynamic learning environment, where ideas are constantly generated and refined. These questions spark creativity, propelling individuals to think beyond conventional boundaries, and envision novel possibilities.
- Mysteries prompt critical thinking and problem-solving. When confronted with uncertainties, individuals within an organization are compelled to analyse, strategize and collaborate to uncover insights and potential solutions. This process hones critical-thinking skills, allowing teams to address challenges more effectively. This approach also nurtures a culture of resilience and adaptability, as teams learn to navigate ambiguity with confidence.
- Unanswered questions fuel innovation. Organizations that view questions as opportunities rather than obstacles are more likely to innovate. The quest for answers can lead to the development of new products, services and processes. Companies like Google and Apple are renowned for their ability to turn unanswered questions into groundbreaking solutions that redefine industries.
- Unsolved mysteries foster a culture of continuous improvement. Organizations that recognize their knowledge gaps are motivated to seek ongoing learning and refinement. This proactive attitude drives organizations to consistently evaluate their practices, adopt new technologies, and evolve to remain competitive in a rapidly changing landscape.

First, a CEO can use unsolved questions to identify new opportunities for growth and innovation. By asking questions that challenge assumptions and push the boundaries of what is currently known, they can identify gaps in the market, untapped customer needs or emerging trends that their organization can capitalize on.

Second, unanswered questions can also be used to drive internal innovation and continuous improvement. By encouraging their teams to ask questions and pursue answers, a CEO can create a culture of curiosity and experimentation that can lead to breakthroughs in product development, process improvement and customer experience.

Third, unsolved mysteries can be a source of inspiration and motivation for employees. By framing them as opportunities for personal and professional growth, a CEO can create a sense of purpose and meaning for their teams. When employees are engaged in solving complex problems, they are more likely to be motivated and invested in the success of the organization.

However, there are also risks in pursuing these questions and mysteries, as stated before. They can be time-consuming and resource-intensive, and may not always yield the desired results. It is up to the CEO to balance the potential benefits with the costs, and make strategic decisions about which unanswered questions to pursue and when.

While striving for solutions is crucial, the power of unsolved mysteries lies in their ability to drive transformation. Organizations that appreciate the significance of uncertainty, and view it as a catalyst for growth, position themselves as pioneers in their industries. By fostering curiosity, critical thinking, collaboration and innovation, these organizations ensure they remain at the forefront of change, continuously evolving and staying relevant in an ever-evolving business landscape.

Ultimately, a CEO's role in using these questions and mysteries to advance their organization is to create a culture of curiosity, experimentation and innovation. By encouraging their teams to ask questions, take risks and pursue answers, a CEO can position their organization to thrive in an ever-changing business landscape.

Like Yudhishthira's hidden power, or Lord Krishna's choice not to invoke it, or Vidura's non-participation, the everyday life of a CEO means traversing myriad situations with complex and paradoxical issues, and no known solutions.

Are faith in a higher power, learning to navigate karmic situations and being resourceful despite the unknown future some of the key characteristics in the life of a CEO's journey? This is something we need to think more about.

Questions that Matter

How can spirituality help individuals connect to a larger purpose, or 'macro cause' in a corporate setting?

Spirituality can be a powerful catalyst for this. While business environments often prioritize profit and performance, the integration of spiritual principles can provide employees with a deeper sense of meaning, alignment with values, and a broader perspective on their contributions.

First, spirituality encourages introspection and self-awareness, enabling individuals to reflect on their personal values and passions. When individuals identify what truly resonates with them, they can align their professional endeavours with a purpose that goes beyond mere job responsibilities. This alignment ignites a sense of fulfilment and commitment, as their work becomes a means of expressing their core beliefs, and contributing to something greater.

Spirituality also nurtures a holistic understanding of success. While financial gains are essential for businesses, spiritual principles broaden the definition of success to encompass ethical conduct, positive impact, and the well-being of all stakeholders. This expanded viewpoint inspires individuals to contribute to a 'macro cause', which aligns with these broader markers of success, creating a sense of purpose beyond financial metrics.

Spiritual practices such as meditation and yoga enhance clarity and focus. This mental clarity enables individuals to envision the bigger picture, and how their efforts fit into the grand scheme of things. Understanding their role in contributing to a larger purpose boosts motivation, as employees recognize the meaningful impact of their work.

What spiritual principles or practices can be used to help employees identify and align with a larger purpose or cause?

There are several principles and practices that can fit the bill.

Gratitude: Ideas such as keeping a gratitude journal or expressing it to colleagues can help employees develop a greater sense of purpose and connection to their work.

Service: Encouraging employees to engage in service, such as volunteering or community service, can help them connect to a larger purpose or cause outside their immediate work environment.

Connection with nature: Encouraging employees to spend time in nature or engage in eco-friendly practices can help them develop a greater sense of connection to the larger ecosystem, and their role in preserving it.

Can any organization seriously develop, implement and pursue a sense of being connected to a larger purpose or cause? Is it practical?

Whether or not an organization can do this depends on a number of factors, including its size and culture, the values of its leaders, and the willingness of employees to engage in such a process.

However, there are a number of benefits that can come from doing so.

Increased employee engagement: When employees feel connected to a larger purpose or cause, they are more likely to be engaged in their work and committed to the organization's success.

Improved productivity: Employees who feel engaged with their work are more likely to be productive.

Increased innovation: Employees who feel connected to a larger purpose or cause are more likely to be innovative and come up with new ideas.

Better decision-making: Connecting to a larger purpose or cause makes employees more likely to make decisions in the best interests of the organization.

Stronger relationships: When employees feel connected to each other, they are more likely to build strong relationships and work together effectively.

One can definitely say that developing a sense of connection to a larger purpose is not only practical, but also highly beneficial for organizations. When aligned with values, intentionally nurtured and effectively communicated, a larger purpose fosters engagement, innovation, resilience and long-term success. Organizations that successfully implement a purpose-driven approach stand to gain a competitive edge in a rapidly changing business landscape.

Is there a reason to believe in a 'larger cause' and 'having a sense of purpose'?

It is better not to persuade anyone, as personal beliefs are deeply individual and to be respected. However, there are reasons why some individuals find profound value in embracing a sense of purpose and connecting with a larger cause.

First, a sense of purpose infuses life with meaning and fulfilment, imparting direction and motivation. Second, such connection fosters a profound sense of belonging, weaving intricate social bonds with like-minded individuals. Third, this sense of purpose propels proactive action, inspiring individuals to contribute positively, not just in their lives, but in others' as well. It is, ultimately, a personal journey, but one that has enriched many lives with purpose and altruism.

Discovering meaning: **Exploring the concept** of a larger cause can open doors to discovering new passions, interests and perspectives that you may not have considered before. This exploration can enrich your life in unexpected ways.

While everyone is entitled to their current beliefs, it's worthwhile to approach the idea of a larger cause and sense of purpose with an open mind. By considering the potential benefits and reflecting on how these concepts might enhance your life, you may find a deeper layer of meaning and fulfilment that you hadn't previously experienced.

Finding your sense of purpose can be a journey, but it's worth going on it. When you know what you're working towards, it can make your life more meaningful and fulfilling.

How can a company align its business objectives with a larger purpose or cause, while still achieving financial success?

Doing this can actually support financial success in the long run, as customers and employees are increasingly drawn to companies that have a positive impact on society and the environment. Here are some ways companies can do so.

Clearly define the company's purpose or cause: The first step in aligning business objectives with a larger purpose or cause is to clearly define what that purpose or cause is. This should be a clear and concise statement that describes the company's mission, values, and the impact it aims to make in the world.

Integrate purpose into the company's strategy: Once the company's purpose or cause has been defined, it should be integrated into the company's overall strategy. This can involve setting specific goals and metrics to measure progress towards the larger purpose or cause.

Balance purpose with financial decision-making: Purpose-driven initiatives should also be financially sustainable. Ensure that the pursuit of the larger cause doesn't jeopardize the company's financial stability.

Engage employees: Getting employees on board with the company's mission is important. This can involve communicating its purpose or cause clearly and regularly, providing opportunities for them to contribute to it, and recognizing and rewarding those who embody the company's values.

When the purpose becomes an integral part of the company's identity and strategy, it not only drives value creation, but also enhances its reputation and ability to attract and retain customers who share the same values.

Is it possible to ensure financial success by integrating spiritual principles in the current situation, where investors and shareholders are always hankering for short-term results?

When investors and shareholders want short-term results, it may be more difficult to integrate spiritual principles. However, it is still possible to do so, and there are a number of companies doing it successfully. By taking a long-term view and focusing on creating a positive and sustainable impact, companies can ensure financial success while also integrating spiritual principles into their business practices.

Here are a few ways to do this.

Creating a culture of engagement and innovation: Integrating spiritual principles can help create a culture where employees feel more engaged, motivated and empowered to innovate. This can result in increased productivity, better customer service and improved product development.

Building brand loyalty: Companies that align their business objectives with a larger purpose or cause are often seen as more trustworthy and authentic by customers. This can result in increased customer loyalty and repeat business, which can drive long-term financial success.

Attracting and retaining top talent: Companies that prioritize spiritual principles and purpose-driven business strategies are often more attractive to job-seekers, particularly those who want meaningful and fulfilling work. This can help companies attract and retain top talent, which can have a positive impact on productivity and the bottom line.

Fostering long-term relationships: Integrating spiritual principles can help companies build stronger and more meaningful relationships with customers, suppliers and other stakeholders. This can lead to greater collaboration, increased trust, and a more supportive business ecosystem, which can support long-term financial success.

Ultimately, the decision of whether or not to integrate spiritual principles in business is up to each individual company. There is no right or wrong answer, and the best approach will vary depending on the specific circumstances.

Chapter Summary

- The pursuit of solving mysteries reflects leaders' courage to delve into uncharted territory, positioning them as pioneers in their fields.
- For those who believe that pursuing unsolved mysteries can lead to failure, the words of Thomas Alva Edison offer some perspective: 'I have not failed 10,000 times; I've successfully found 10,000 ways that will not work.'
- To grow stronger, leaders must continually challenge the status quo (the devil you know) and step out of their comfort zones,.

This transformation is attainable only through pursuing unsolved mysteries.
- This pursuit demands equilibrium of curiosity and creativity. Curiosity by itself can kill the proverbial cat.
- In a sense, this persistent inquisitive mindset guides leaders towards discovering the ultimate cause over time, helping them realize a greater purpose.

9

Strong People Skills and Empathy

mātrā-sparśhās tu kaunteya śhītoṣhṇa-sukha-duḥkha-dāḥ
āgamāpāyino 'nityās tans-titikṣhasva bhārata

(O son of Kunti, the contact between the senses and objects gives rise to fleeting perceptions of happiness and distress. These are impermanent like the winter and summer. O descendent of Bharat, one must learn to tolerate them without being disturbed.)
—Bhagavad Gita, chapter 2, verse 14

Context

The most significant aspect of being a leader is first managing one's own emotions, and then assisting team members with theirs. If a leader can inspire team members to navigate the ups and downs of the corporate world in a mature manner, half the battle is won.

The ability to understand the emotions of team members is a critical factor for a leader's success.

Prelude

Strong people skills and empathy are essential for success in any field, but they hold particular importance in the workplace. Individuals with strong people skills can build relationships, communicate effectively, and resolve conflicts. Moreover, they possess the ability to comprehend and value the perspectives of others.

Empathy, on the other hand, involves understanding and sharing the emotions of another person. It is a crucial element for establishing trust and rapport with others.

These two qualities are crucial for the following reasons:

Building relationships: Leaders need to forge robust relationships with employees, customers, partners and other stakeholders. Empathy and strong people skills assist leaders in establishing connections, comprehending people's needs and concerns, and fostering trust.

Team management: Effective team management is essential to achieving organizational goals. Strong people skills enable leaders to inspire and motivate team members, encourage collaboration and communication, and resolve conflicts.

Customer satisfaction: This is a pivotal factor in an organization's success. Empathy helps leaders comprehend customers' needs and expectations, enabling them to design products and services that cater to those needs.

Change management: Navigating the path to an organization's future often involves substantial changes. Empathy and strong people skills facilitate effective communication of changes, addressing employee concerns and ensuring a seamless transition.

Innovation: This is vital for maintaining competitiveness and growth. Leaders need to cultivate an innovative culture, requiring strong people skills and empathy to encourage risk-taking, creativity and experimentation.

A dearth of people skills and empathy in a leader can have a significant negative impact on the workplace environment, employee engagement and overall organizational performance. Therefore, leaders must develop these skills to foster positive relationships, cultivate a healthy workplace culture, and achieve success.

Yaksha Prashna

Now, I'll share one of my favourite stories from the Mahabharata—how will Dharma, that is Yudhishthira, respond in a life-or-death situation that will test all his skills?

The story takes place towards the end of the twelfth year of the Pandavas' exile, with one more year of agyatvasa (living incognito) coming up soon.

The Pandavas are sitting and talking at the edge of the forest, when a priest arrives and requests help. He says an antlered deer has taken away the wooden blocks he uses to light a fire, and so, he can't begin his rituals. Yudhishthira, true to his benevolent, kingly nature, agrees to help.

The Pandavas set out into the forest to find the deer, but after chasing success for a long time, they get tired and thirsty. They find a place to rest, and Yudhishthira asks Nakula to find some drinking water. Nakula goes into the forest, and finds a pond. But before he can get water from it, a stork rises from the centre of the pond and starts speaking to him. 'O Nakula, please answer my questions before you can take water from the pond, else you will be dead.'

Nakula laughs recklessly, thinking what can a bird do to him? He takes the water for his brothers, and drinks some himself. But as soon as he drinks the water, he drops dead; the water is poisonous.

When Nakula doesn't return for a long time, Yudhishthira sends his twin brother Sahadeva after him. Sahadeva arrives at the pond and is baffled to find his brother dead. He also goes to take the water, but drops dead too when he refuses to answer the stork's questions and drinks the water. Arjuna and Bhima also arrive and meet the same fate.

With none of his brothers returning, Yudhishthira goes looking for them, and finds them all dead by the pond. He doesn't know what befell them, but then, the stork appears and begins talking to him. When the stork tells him to answer its questions, Yudhishthira realizes it holds the clues to his brothers' deaths. So, he agrees to answer the questions, and the creature takes into its true form—a yaksha (nature spirit).

The yaksha poses about 125 questions on philosophy, many dharmic concepts and values, gods, etc. You can look them all up if you want, but there is one question that assumed the greatest importance, and came to be known as 'Yaksha Prashna'.

'What is the strangest thing in this world?' the yaksha asks.

Yudhishthira responds: 'The strangest thing is that people around us are falling dead all the time, and yet man thinks he's going to live eternally.'

The yaksha is pleased with Yudhishthira's answers, and says, 'my hands are now bound to dharma'. But it adds that it can only resurrect one of his brothers, so he has to make a choice. Yudhishthira thinks for a while and says, 'please resurrect Nakula'.

The yaksha is surprised that even though there is an impending war, Yudhishthira isn't choosing the strongest warriors in Bhima or Arjuna. It asks: 'Would you mind telling me what made you choose Nakula?'

Yudhishthira says: 'The name which I stand for, Dharma, is what made me choose him, because I am born of Kunti and so are Bhima and Arjuna, whereas Nakula and Sahadeva are born of my stepmother Madri. There has to be a balance in the family. Thus, I chose Nakula, so that his mother, in her memory, would have a son who lives on.'

The yaksha is so happy with the answer that he now reveals himself as Yama, the god of death, and Yudhishthira's father. He was also disguised as the deer which took away the wooden blocks in its antlers.

'I am so happy with the choice you made, because you have established exactly what dharma stands for,' Yama says, and brings all the Pandavas back to life. He also blesses them and assures that on their one-year agyatvasa, he will protect them and ensure they aren't found by the Kauravas.

How the Tale Connects to the Corporate World

This story provides profound insights into the essence of dharma, the personification of which is Yudhishthira. Whether you're a sibling, a family member, a corporate executive, a national leader or someone heading a political or religious organization, what dharma will you uphold? What did dharma signify in this context? What choices did Yudhishthira have? How did he, in awfully challenging circumstances, find what seems to be the middle path? He would have had the urge to engage in conflict, and he also possessed considerable power.

Yet, Yudhishthira followed obedience when he entered the realm of the yaksha, respecting its rules, and answered its questions patiently.

This tale introduces various dimensions of inquiry related to administration, leadership and the values one must uphold. It presents a series of values and dharma that Yudhishthira skillfully demonstrated, which are pivotal in upholding the fabric of dharma. Upholding dharma necessitates strong people skills and empathy. Yudhishthira chose people over power, a decision that ultimately restored his authority and aided him in winning the war. His act of choosing his stepbrother Nakula over the stronger Bhima or Arjuna illustrates his empathy and remarkable people skills.

The tale of the Yaksha Prashna imparts a valuable lesson to leaders of all types, even in contemporary times. It underscores that leaders must possess wisdom and fairness, and consistently act in accordance with dharma. It also underscores the importance of quick thinking, and the ability to make tough decisions for leaders.

There are three key lessons that leaders can readily take away from this story:

Wisdom: Yudhishthira's ability to provide accurate answers to the challenging questions posed by the yaksha showcases his understanding of what is just. In real life, followers also want their leaders to be equitable and just.

Impartial justice: Followers expect their leaders to exhibit the same fairness Yudhishthira did in his equitable and impartial approach. He did not resort to deception or manipulation; he was willing to accept the outcomes without showing any partiality or emotion.

Decision-making: Yudhishthira's capacity to swiftly make tough decisions in high-pressure situations stands out. When challenged by the yaksha, he didn't hesitate, and was able to provide accurate responses. Moreover, he also showcases qualities like being an attentive listener, being decisive, truthful and just.

Take a moment to reflect on the dharmic values conveyed by this story, and consider how these values can be integrated into our daily lives. By incorporating such values, we can effect personal transformation and contribute to societal change, moving towards a higher set of values.

Questions that Matter

How can spirituality help individuals develop strong people skills and empathy in a corporate setting?

Spirituality can play a transformative role in this. Here's how:

Fostering inclusivity: Spirituality highlights the interconnectedness of all beings. Individuals who embrace this perspective are more likely to value diversity and inclusivity, creating an environment where differences are celebrated and respected.

Encouraging collaboration: It can promote a sense of interdependence, which can help individuals see the value of collaboration and teamwork. This can lead to more effective problem-solving and decision-making in a corporate setting.

Here are some specific examples.

- A manager mindful of their employees' needs is more likely to create a positive and supportive work environment.

- A compassionate salesperson is more likely to build trust and rapport with their customers.
- A forgiving leader is more likely to create a team that is cohesive and productive.
- A patient negotiator is more likely to reach a mutually beneficial agreement.
- A grateful employee is more likely to be motivated and engaged in their work.

What spiritual principles or practices can be used to help employees cultivate empathy and improve their ability to connect with others?

While business environments often prioritize tasks and outcomes, integrating spiritual principles can lead to more compassionate and effective interpersonal interactions. Here are a few ways to achieve this:

Meditation: This can help focus attention on and become more aware of our thoughts and feelings, which could make us more mindful of others, leading to understand their perspectives.

Self-awareness: Spiritual practices encourage self-reflection and self-awareness. Individuals who engage in practices like meditation and mindfulness gain insight into their own emotions, thoughts and behaviours. This heightened self-awareness enables them to recognize their biases, triggers and communication patterns, allowing for more conscious and empathetic interactions with others.

How can a company promote a culture of empathy and compassion while also achieving business objectives?

This is both achievable and advantageous. Such a culture not only enhances employee well-being, but also contributes to enhanced collaboration, innovation, and overall business success.

Here are some specific examples of how companies can promote such a culture.

- Establish clear policies and procedures that promote respect and understanding. This could include policies against bullying, discrimination and harassment.
- Provide training on empathy and compassion for all employees. This could cover topics such as active listening, conflict resolution and emotional intelligence.
- Create opportunities for employees to connect with each other on a personal level. This could be done through team-building activities, social events or mentoring programmes.
- Recognize and reward employees for acts of empathy and compassion. This shows employees that the company values these qualities, and encourages them to continue to demonstrate them.
- Establish mentoring programmes that pair experienced employees with newcomers. This provides a platform for sharing experiences, advice and fostering connections built on empathy.
- Create an inclusive environment that values diverse perspectives. Encourage dialogue about different experiences and backgrounds, promoting empathy and understanding.
- Implement well-being programmes that focus on mental, emotional and physical health. Prioritizing employees' well-being is a direct reflection of empathy and care.

A culture that prioritizes employee well-being and interpersonal connection often leads to improved teamwork, higher employee engagement and greater overall success in achieving business goals.

Does spirituality help leaders and managers develop strong people skills and become more effective communicators and collaborators? How?

Yes, when spiritual principles are integrated into leadership practices, they foster self-awareness, empathy and a deep sense of connection with others, leading to enhanced interpersonal skills. Here's how spirituality can contribute practically to these areas.

- It can help leaders and managers be more mindful of others, which would make them more likely to be aware of their needs and feelings, and that could lead to more empathy and better relationships.
- It can help leaders and managers to be more compassionate, which would make them more likely to care about the well-being of others, and that could lead to more understanding and support.
- It can help leaders and managers become more forgiving, which would make them more likely to let go of anger and resentment, and that could lead to more positive relationships with others.
- It can help leaders and managers become more patient, which would make them more likely to take the time to understand others, and that could build better communication and trust.
- It can help leaders and managers grow more grateful, which would make them more likely to appreciate the good things in life, and that could lead to more positivity and optimism.

Here are some specific examples of how spirituality can help leaders and managers develop strong people skills and become more effective communicators and collaborators.

- A heartful leader is more likely to be aware of the needs of their employees, and to create a supportive work environment.
- A compassionate leader is more likely to be understanding and supportive of their employees, even when they make mistakes.
- A forgiving leader is more likely to create a positive and productive work environment, as employees feel less stressed and more confident in taking risks.
- A patient leader is more likely to listen to their employees and to build trust.
- A grateful leader is more likely to be positive and optimistic, which can create a more positive work environment for everyone.

Could a people-focused culture and building a sense of empathy counter efforts to boost productivity and profitability?

No, on the contrary, research has shown that these can actually help boost productivity and profitability in several ways.

- First, a people-focused culture can improve employee engagement and motivation, which leads to increased productivity. When employees feel valued, respected and supported, they are more likely to be invested in their work and go above and beyond to achieve their goals.
- Second, such a culture can lead to improved customer satisfaction and loyalty. When employees are trained to be empathetic and

provide excellent customer service, customers are more likely to have a positive experience and bring more business.
- Third, a people-focused culture can improve teamwork and collaboration, which can lead to better problem-solving and decision-making. When employees feel a sense of connection and trust with their colleagues, they are more likely to work together effectively, and share ideas and perspectives.

I recently read a story that links certain elements together. During that era (in India). District collectors, after their selection, couldn't directly take over that role and responsibility. Instead, they were required to initiate their journey from the clerk's desk. After spending a fair amount of time comprehending the processes, they would proceed to the next desk, moving up through each level before eventually assuming the collector's position. This approach enabled them to grasp the challenges and intricacies faced by the team at each level, fostering a deep sense of empathy. Ultimately, this method cultivates robust interpersonal skills, before the selected individual finally steps into the collector's role.

While a people-focused culture may require an initial investment of time and resources, the long-term benefits can be significant in terms of improved productivity, profitability, and employee and customer retention.

Chapter Summary

- Leaders who genuinely exhibit empathy toward others are the ones equipped with strong people skills.
- From personal experience, I can assert that when leaders invest in building connections with people through empathy, those same people reciprocate with trust, reverence, love and empathy.

- Leaders possessing robust people skills have the capacity to intuitively understand and resonate with their team's feelings and needs even before explicit communication.
- While many individuals within organizations tend to resist change, leaders endowed with exceptional people skills emerge as catalysts, skillfully guiding the journey through change.
- The strong people skills displayed by leaders also denote an open-hearted, open-minded approach coupled with respect for their team, acting as genuine boosters and sources of encouragement.

10

High on Values and Integrity: Dharma vs Swadharma

nainaṁ chhindanti śhastrāṇi nainaṁ dahati pāvakaḥ na chainaṁ kledayantyāpo na śhoṣhayati mārutaḥ

(Weapons cannot shred the soul, nor can fire burn it. Water cannot wet it, nor can the wind dry it.)
—Bhagavad Gita, chapter 2, verse 23

Context

Lord Krishna alludes to the concept of integrity through the example of the soul, which remains unaffected by external influences. The presence or absence of integrity within an individual carries significant weight. But what precisely constitutes integrity, and why is it held in such high regard?

Integrity involves harmonizing one's actions with their values, and consistently upholding them. This is a challenging endeavour, as external pressures often drag us off course. Numerous actions stand as indicators of a person's integrity. Examples from the corporate realm include refraining from discussing absent colleagues, not making unwarranted promises of promotion, abstaining from disparaging peers to further personal gain, not manipulating data, handling available funds responsibly and honouring confidentiality agreements.

Prelude

Values and integrity hold paramount importance for a leader, as they establish a bedrock of trust and respect. When leaders possess steadfast values, they tend to make decisions that prioritize the welfare of their followers. Additionally, they are more inclined to engage in honest and transparent interactions with others.

Integrity, characterized by honesty and robust moral principles, significantly contributes to a leader's ability to garner the trust of their followers. Such leaders are also esteemed for their unwavering dedication to ethical conduct.

To be high on values and integrity signifies a person will not prioritize their personal gain, and make decisions and take actions according to these values even in the face of challenges or opposition.

For leaders, this involves embodying and upholding the values integral to the organization they lead. They set an exemplar for others to follow, and base their decisions on the organization's values, vision and mission. This fosters a culture characterized by integrity, ethical conduct and accountability throughout the organization.

Integrity serves as a cornerstone of effective leadership, reflecting the congruence between a leader's actions, values and words with their ethical standards and moral principles.

Maintaining a high level of values and integrity holds paramount importance because it sets the organizational tone. This sets the groundwork for fostering a culture characterized by ethical behaviour, integrity and accountability across all levels.

Here are some specific instances:

- A leader who prizes honesty is more inclined to maintain transparency with their team, and uphold their commitments. This can lay the foundation for trust and loyalty.
- A leader who esteems fairness is more likely to treat every individual equitably and provide equal opportunities. This contributes to fostering a sense of justice and impartiality.
- A leader who values courage is more apt to stand up for their convictions, even when facing opposition. This can ignite a spark of courage within others.
- A leader who treasures compassion is more predisposed to be empathetic and supportive toward their team. This fosters a nurturing and positive work environment.

Values and integrity are indispensable for leaders in building trust, credibility, and a conducive organizational culture. By consistently exemplifying ethical conduct, prioritizing transparency and nurturing an environment of accountability, leaders can inspire their teams to embrace similar values and actively contribute to the organization's long-term success.

We will now delve into a captivating story that is not exactly considered 'canon'; it's more of an urban legend that features in several renditions of the Mahabharata.

The source of the titular last temptation of Karna is none other than Lord Krishna himself.

Karna's Last Temptation

Approximately a week before the commencement of the war in Kurukshetra, Krishna visits Karna and invites him to join him in his chariot. Krishna enquires about Karna's awareness of his birth and related matters. In a twist that those familiar with the Mahabharata would recognize, Karna is fully cognizant of his origins and how he came into the world. He was born to the Pandavas' mother, Kunti, and because she wasn't yet married, she had no choice but to abandon him as an infant.

Now, Lord Krishna tempts Karna, telling him it is an established dharmic practice that even if a son is born prior to his mother entering into wedlock, after her marriage, he becomes the son of her husband. And since Kunti later married Pandu, according to the prevailing shastras of the time, Karna is a Pandava. Krishna explains that this battle is part of his dharma, or duty. He must not hesitate or later regret his actions when the consequences become clear. His responsibility is to act, not to question the outcome.

Now, Lord Krishna says: 'Imagine that you side with the Pandavas. There is still time for the war to begin, and the Pandavas would be happy to have you on their side. You know that Pandavas are going to win this war, even before it has begun. Yudhishthira would happily accept you as his older brother, and the Pandavas, once they win the war, will rule all the known parts of the earth, making you the undisputed king of the world. You will have at your side the mighty Bhima, Arjuna, Nakula and Sahadeva, alongside the renowned warriors of the Pandava lineage. History will remember you as someone who understood and rectified the error.'

Krishna goes on to offer more advice and insights. But Karna responds beautifully.

'Krishna, I am aware about what you are saying in terms of global and universal dharma. I'm sorry for whatever I've done to the Pandavas by being with the Kauravas, beside my dear friend Duryodhana. But please look at it from the point of view of my swadharma. As I see it, I was abandoned as a child. My mother forsook me though after her marriage to Pandu, she could have easily told the truth and brought me back into the fold. But she did not. I was repeatedly insulted throughout my life. My foster mother loved and cared for me so much that she was able to breastfeed me like her own son. When I grew up, the entire world would persistently make fun of me, before I met Duryodhana. There was no hidden agenda in his love and affection for me. He saw in me something that others failed to. He did not see the upcoming war; he did not manipulate or calculate that having Karna on his side would be of help,' Karna says.

'Duryodhana saw me as a person who was downtrodden. He saw the ability of a Kshatriya in me and brought me to his side. He kept me there in spite of all the challenges thrown by elders like Kripacharya, Dronacharya and Bhishma, none of whom accepted me. After all this, when it is time for war, and just because I have found my biological roots now, if I go back, I will be slipping from my duty as a person who wants to uphold swadharma. To me, holding up my values is more important than what you would call dharma. I know the war will end in favour of the Pandavas; I am certain that I will get killed by Arjuna; and also that all the stalwarts who are on the side of the Kauravas will get defeated because they are on the other side of dharma. And this is being led by none other than Lord Krishna himself. What more can I ask for?' he continues.

'I also know that you have a grand plan to cleanse the entire system. These people, unless they die in this war, may not be able to reach heaven in this lifetime or subsequent ones. I do have a certain foresight into what you have planned. If I were to change the situation by switching sides, it is possible that the war may not take place, because I'm sure that Duryodhana would be crestfallen, and his side will accept defeat. In that case, the war will not serve the purpose for which you have devised it. Thus, if I give up swadharma for the sake of the dharma that you are representing, the dharmic equilibrium that you want to restore in this world by killing many kings and warriors will not happen. Hence, kindly accept my apologies.'

Lord Krishna remarks: 'I have bestowed upon you everything, and even assured you of my support. I'm genuinely delighted and astonished by your commitment to your swadharma.'

Then, a remarkable sequence unfolds. Karna requests that the same boons he's been granted be extended to all those who will lose their lives on the battlefield—every individual, regardless of their allegiance in the conflict, should find their way to heaven and welcomed. Even if aware of Krishna's plan, Karna's request could serve to reinforce this outcome on behalf of all warriors and perhaps demonstrate his own virtue. Lord Krishna grants Karna's request, and as a result, all those who perish on the battlefield are able to go to heaven.

How This Tale Connects to the Corporate World

Dharma and swadharma are two pivotal concepts within Hindu philosophy—dharma signifies the universal law or order that governs the cosmos, whereas swadharma pertains to an individual's responsibilities or societal role derived from their innate nature, capabilities and circumstances.

When faced with the choice between dharma and swadharma, the general belief is that dharma should take precedence, because it represents the overarching moral duty that applies to all individuals.

It is regarded as a loftier ethical obligation that supersedes personal duties and desires.

For instance, if an individual's swadharma means engaging in an activity that contradicts the universal moral principles of dharma, they should prioritize the latter and abstain from such an activity that could inflict harm on others, or breach ethical standards.

However, it's crucial to recognize that dharma and swadharma need not be in perpetual conflict. In reality, an individual's swadharma is believed to align harmoniously with universal dharma, and adhering to it is seen as a means to fulfil personal duties and contribute to the greater welfare of society.

Indeed, the interplay between dharma and swadharma is a nuanced topic in ethical and philosophical discourse. While dharma is frequently underscored as a guiding principle, situations may arise where an individual must prioritize their swadharma over universal moral principles. This nuanced perspective acknowledges the intricacy of human experiences and ethical decision-making.

Here are some instances where swadharma might take precedence:

Balancing personal obligations: Swadharma pertains to an individual's specific duty or role in life. Occasionally, they may encounter conflicting moral choices in adhering to it, such as family responsibilities or personal commitments, which could make them temporarily diverge from universal dharma. Balancing these obligations necessitates thoughtful consideration.

Cultural, social and contextual variations: These factors can exert influence over ethical considerations. What is universally regarded as dharma might exhibit variability across cultures, and in such instances, following one's swadharma might serve as a means to navigate intricate cultural landscapes without compromising core values.

Self-care and well-being: Prioritizing swadharma could be essential when it encompasses self-care, mental well-being or overall health. Occasionally, individuals may need to step back from customary duties to ensure personal health, thereby enabling them to better fulfil both personal and moral obligations in the long term.

Flexibility in ethical dilemmas: Life presents intricate ethical dilemmas. When tension between dharma and swadharma surfaces, individuals might need to seek a balance that aligns with their values and immediate responsibilities.

Unique life circumstances: Every individual's life circumstances are distinctive. What constitutes a universal moral principle in one context might necessitate adaptation to suit an individual's situation. This adaptability underscores the dynamic nature of ethical decision-making.

However, it's also crucial to recognize that instances where swadharma takes precedence don't diminish the significance of adhering to universal dharma; rather, they underscore the intricacy of ethical decisions and the need for meticulous evaluation in each circumstance. The solution to this quandary lies in a considerate approach that factors in individual duties and broader moral principles, aiming for harmony whenever feasible.

Ultimately, resolving the conflict between swadharma and dharma is a personal undertaking. There exists no definitive right or wrong answer, and the optimal route is often found by paying heed to your heart and following your conscience—both of which usually guide you effectively, if you know how to listen!

In the Karna story, how should swadharma operate, even though it conflicts with dharma? Should it be independent of broader dharmic principles, or align strictly with them?

Often in our own lives, we find ourselves aligned with our personal values even if they don't align with global values. In such cases, how should we perceive this misalignment? Is friendship more profound than blood ties? This story prompts numerous inquiries of this nature.

As a leader or CEO, you will inevitably encounter challenging situations where you must choose between dharma and swadharma. While this story provides one perspective—Karna's—your circumstances may differ substantially.

Questions That Matter

What spiritual principles or practices can be used to help employees stay true to their values and maintain their integrity, even in difficult or testing situations?

In the modern corporate landscape, this can be a daunting task. However, integrating spiritual principles and practices into the workplace can provide employees with a solid foundation for navigating such situations while staying true to their values. By fostering self-awareness, empathy, resilience and ethical decision-making, individuals can be empowered to uphold their integrity, contribute positively to their organizations, and build a healthier work environment.

Here are some principles and practices that can help:

Resilience and acceptance: Spiritual teachings often emphasize the importance of accepting and learning from adversity. Encouraging employees to develop resilience helps them bounce back from setbacks, maintaining their integrity and values even when faced with difficulties. Embracing challenges as opportunities for growth rather than as obstacles can foster a mindset that is resilient in the face of ethical dilemmas.

Ethical decision-making: Integrating frameworks inspired by spiritual principles can guide employees through complex situations. They often involve contemplating the potential consequences of actions on oneself and others, aligning decisions with core values and seeking guidance from mentors or trusted individuals. Encouraging open dialogue about ethical dilemmas and providing avenues for seeking advice can help employees make principled choices.

Purpose and meaning: Connecting work to a greater sense of purpose and meaning is a key component of many spiritual traditions. Encouraging employees to understand how their roles contribute to the organization's larger mission can reinforce their commitment to values and integrity. When employees perceive their work as meaningful, they are more likely to uphold their principles, even in challenging circumstances.

Authentic communication: Spiritual principles often emphasize encouraging open and transparent communication in the workplace. This fosters an environment where employees feel safe expressing their concerns and dilemmas. This allows for collective problem-solving and finding solutions that align with shared values.

How can a company promote a culture of high values and integrity among employees, and yet make them accountable?

Imagine a company that embodies its values and integrity not just as a set of rules, but as a living, breathing culture that inspires accountability at every level. To achieve this, the company could embrace a dynamic approach that melds creativity, technology and human psychology, resulting in an innovative and engaging way to foster high values and accountability. Here are some ways how:

Narrative-based ethics: Instead of traditional rule-based ethics, the company could create a narrative-driven ethical framework. Craft a compelling company story that illustrates the real-world impact of decisions aligned with its values, and those that deviate from them. Use storytelling to connect employees emotionally with the outcomes of their actions, highlighting the importance of integrity. This approach transforms ethics from a set of abstract principles to a relatable and memorable journey, making employees more accountable for their choices.

Virtual reality ethical simulations: Immerse employees in virtual reality simulations that present them with challenging ethical dilemmas. This tech-savvy approach allows employees to navigate complex situations and experience the consequences of their decisions in a safe environment. By observing how their choices influence outcomes, employees become more attuned to the importance of maintaining integrity while being held accountable for their virtual actions.

Blockchain-backed integrity badges: Leverage blockchain technology to create integrity badges that employees can earn and showcase. These badges could represent milestones achieved through consistent ethical behaviour. As employees accumulate badges, they not only signal their commitment to high values, but also become part of a visible community that celebrates integrity. This approach makes accountability a literal badge of honour, and fosters healthy competition to embody company values.

Collaborative transparent metrics: Transform accountability into a team effort by introducing transparent performance metrics that measure not only traditional goals, but also ethical performance. Collaborative goal-setting and progress-tracking encourage employees to support each other in upholding values. This approach transforms accountability from a top-down mandate to a shared responsibility, where colleagues hold each other accountable for maintaining integrity.

Innovative whistleblowing mechanism: Reinvent the traditional whistleblower system by creating an anonymous platform that utilizes artificial intelligence to analyse patterns and detect potential breaches of integrity. By offering a safe space to report concerns, employees feel empowered to uphold values and hold others accountable without fear of retaliation. This approach ensures accountability while building trust and a sense of shared responsibility.

How can spirituality help leaders and managers set an example of high values and integrity for their employees?

Spirituality is the belief in a higher power, or a sense of connection to something larger than oneself. It can be a source of strength, guidance and inspiration for many people. In the realm of leadership, where balancing organizational goals with ethical considerations is paramount, integrating spirituality in unconventional ways can serve as a potent catalyst for fostering a culture of high values and integrity. By transcending conventional paradigms and embracing spiritual principles, leaders can set an example that resonates deeply with their employees, fostering a harmonious and values-driven workplace.

Contemplative leadership retreats: Imagine leaders embarking on immersive, contemplative retreats that blend meditation, introspection and reflection practices with leadership development. These experiences allow leaders to connect with their inner selves, cultivating self-awareness and empathy. When leaders model authentic self-awareness and empathy, employees witness firsthand the power of these qualities, inspiring them to integrate similar practices into their own professional lives.

Ethical story circles: Leaders could gather their teams in circles to share personal stories of ethical dilemmas they've faced, emphasizing the decision-making processes they used to align with their values. This narrative-based approach humanizes leaders, making them relatable and approachable. By showcasing their vulnerability and commitment to values, leaders demonstrate that ethical considerations are central to decision-making.

Mentorship from diverse spiritual traditions: This exposure broadens leaders' perspectives on values and integrity, enabling them to integrate a diverse array of ethical principles into their leadership style. This multidimensional approach cultivates leaders who can guide their teams with wisdom that transcends cultural boundaries.

Values-driven innovation labs: Leaders could establish innovation labs focused on generating novel solutions aligned with the company's values to societal or environmental challenges. This approach merges spirituality with innovation, demonstrating how ethical principles can drive positive change. As leaders guide employees through these labs, they show that high values and integrity are not just abstract concepts, but integral to pioneering change.

Reflective decision-making journals: Leaders could encourage employees to maintain reflective journals that document their decision-making processes in alignment with values. Leaders can share their own journals openly, showcasing how they navigate complex decisions while upholding integrity. This practice transforms leadership into a transparent journey, fostering mutual learning and respect.

Values-centred leadership awards: Imagine an unconventional awards ceremony, celebrating leaders who exemplify high values and integrity. This event could incorporate artistic performances, storytelling and collaborative discussions around ethical leadership. By showcasing and celebrating these role models, the company can emphasize that values-driven leadership is not just an expectation, but a commendable achievement.

This innovative fusion of spirituality and leadership empowers both leaders and employees to navigate the complex terrain of business while staying anchored to their shared values.

How does integrating spirituality impact the organization's culture? Does it help achieve business success, as well as a reputation for a strong commitment to values and integrity and never compromising during testing situations?

Imagine an organization where spirituality is interwoven into the DNA, creating a transformative impact that reverberates through every facet of its existence. This not only cultivates a reputation for unwavering commitment to values and integrity, but also serves as a catalyst for business success, even in the face of challenges. In this unconventional approach, spirituality becomes the driving force behind sustainable success and an unyielding ethical compass.

Elevated employee engagement and well-being: When spirituality is nurtured within the organization, employees experience a profound sense of purpose and interconnectedness. This results in higher levels of engagement, job satisfaction and overall well-being. Employees who feel spiritually aligned with the company's values are more likely to invest their energy and creativity into their work, leading to increased productivity and innovation.

Resilience in testing situations: Spirituality equips individuals with resilience in the face of adversity. When an organization's culture is infused with spiritual principles such as mindfulness, empathy and acceptance, employees are better equipped to navigate testing situations without compromising their integrity. This resilience stems from the deep well of inner strength cultivated through spiritual practices, enabling employees to make principled decisions under pressure.

Enhanced collaboration and trust: Spirituality fosters empathy, compassion and authentic communication. In an organization where these qualities are prioritized, collaboration flourishes. Employees interact with one another based on mutual respect and a deep understanding of each other's perspectives. This heightened trust leads to effective teamwork, streamlined processes, and ultimately, better business outcomes.

Innovation rooted in purpose: Integrating spirituality into the organization's culture provides a fertile ground for innovative thinking. Employees who are connected to a sense of purpose beyond profit are more likely to devise innovative solutions that address societal and environmental challenges. These purpose-driven innovations not only elevate the organization's brand but also contribute positively to the world.

Attracting and retaining top talent: Organizations known for their commitment to values and integrity become magnets for top talent seeking a meaningful workplace. When spirituality is part of the equation, potential employees are drawn to an environment that aligns with their personal values, leading to a more engaged and dedicated workforce. Moreover, existing employees are more likely to stay loyal to an organization that respects their holistic well-being.

Long-term sustainability: An organization steeped in spirituality is naturally inclined towards long-term sustainability. By placing value on interconnectedness and a sense of responsibility towards the broader community and environment, the organization makes choices that are not only profitable in the short term, but also sustainable in the long run. This sustainability resonates with stakeholders, fostering lasting trust and support.

Chapter Summary

- Leaders possessing a high level of integrity, marked by strong adherence to values, are in sync with themselves, and consequently, with their teams and customers. This alignment fosters harmony, which in turn cultivates inner peace, ultimately leading to clarity of thought at each stage.
- Integrity involves the alignment of one's thoughts, actions, and deeds with the values to which one is deeply committed.
- Integrity acts as the cornerstone upon which individuals and leaders construct their character. However, rather than being flaunted, this foundation should be nurtured in the shadows.
- Organizations constructed under the guidance of leaders with unwavering integrity represent the true reservoirs of brand value and goodwill that endure the test of time, propelling them to the pinnacle of success.
- In the presence of leaders who exemplify integrity and uphold high values, resistance—whether originating from within or without—becomes futile.

11

Baker's Dozen

Bakers in medieval England often faced penalties for providing customers with insufficient weight of goods. But even with careful planning, it was difficult to ensure all the goods came out the same size. Afraid that they would be found short and flogged, bakers would throw in a bit of extra dough into every baked good, or give thirteen items to the dozen. The term 'baker's dozen' has therefore come to mean thirteen, one more than the usual dozen, that is twelve.

I have deliberately chosen this title to highlight that I'm putting particulars or anecdotes in this chapter that have not been mentioned previously. This selection guarantees the comprehensive coverage of all pertinent information.

Epigenetics, Spirituality and Leadership: Unveiling Hidden Connections

In the realm of leadership, the integration of science and spirituality has been a long-explored subject. Epigenetics, an emerging field of study, has illuminated the interplay between our genetic makeup and external influences, while spirituality has guided leaders in connecting with a higher purpose. There exists an intriguing junction between epigenetics, spirituality and leadership, which can have a profound impact on personal growth and organizational success.

Epigenetics stands as a captivating and revolutionary domain of research, challenging conventional notions about genetics and inheritance. Bruce Lipton, biologist and author, is a pivotal figure in the field. Lipton's work has significantly propelled the notion of epigenetics into the scientific and public spotlight. Let us delve into the symbiotic relationship between epigenetics and leadership.

Traditionally, genetics has been associated with the belief that our traits and attributes are solely dictated by the DNA sequence inherited from our parents. However, epigenetics offers a more intricate and dynamic perspective. Epigenetic mechanisms involve alterations to the DNA molecule or its associated proteins that can modulate gene expression without altering the DNA sequence itself. These modifications act as switches, activating or deactivating genes, thus determining the expression of our genes and the functionality of our cells.

Lipton, in his book *The Biology of Belief*, introduces the concept of 'new biology', which challenges the conventional notion that genes exert complete control over us. He posits that the environment—inclusive of our thoughts, beliefs and perceptions—primarily shapes gene expression, ultimately influencing our physical and emotional well-being.

Lipton's exploration of cell biology and epigenetics has revealed that the cellular membrane, rather than the nucleus, serves as the primary site for receiving environmental signals. These signals wield the power to influence the cell's response and patterns of gene expression. He suggests that through altering our beliefs and attitudes, we possess the capability to create a more positive internal environment, consequently fostering enhanced health and overall well-being.

The findings carry extensive implications within the spheres of personal empowerment and leadership. Lipton's research indicates that we possess more control over our physical and mental health and our destiny than previously conceived. Through embracing positive lifestyle values and choices, adept stress management, and the creation of a nurturing cellular environment, we can significantly influence our gene expression and overall well-being.

Furthermore, Lipton's insights have spurred the emergence of a new paradigm in the medical field, accentuating the significance of integrative approaches that encompass both physical and emotional facets of health. This comprehensive view acknowledges the intricate interplay between the mind, body and surroundings, advocating a holistic perspective on healthcare and individual well-being. This dynamic rings particularly true in the arena of leadership. Indeed, epigenetics is markedly shaping our cognitive landscape and our very essence—our amalgamation of dharma, karma and swadharma (DKS).

Epigenetics, in tandem with Bruce Lipton's pioneering contributions, has shattered the conventional deterministic outlook on genetics, replacing it with an empowering stance on human biology. Similarly, DKS together are challenging the notion that businesses are solely driven by profit motives, with values and purpose relegated to secondary roles. Just as epigenetics possesses the potential to sculpt our biological trajectory, fostering healthier and more enriching lives, the concepts of DKS are orchestrating a transformative impact in the realm of Leadership. They elucidate that human existence transcends our prevailing corporate convictions, encompassing a profound interconnectedness with other people and the vast universe.

Numerous accomplished leaders draw from spiritual practices to heighten their self-awareness, empathy and emotional intelligence. Nurturing spirituality enables these leaders to establish an authentic, compassionate and purpose-driven connection with their inner selves. This holistic leadership approach cultivates an atmosphere of trust, collaboration and mutual advancement within organizations—a milieu where performance is predicated on purpose rather than pressure.

The Enlightened Leader

Let us meet Alex, a seasoned executive grappling with the complex challenges of modern leadership. Amid the relentless pressures of achieving corporate triumph, Alex felt a profound disconnect with both personal values and team dynamics. The struggle to ignite inspiration within the workforce compelled Alex to recognize the necessity for a metamorphosis.

In a determined pursuit to rediscover purpose and significance, Alex participated in a leadership retreat, delving into the confluence of epigenetics, spirituality and effective leadership. Throughout this retreat, Alex garnered insights into the influence of stress on gene expression and the paramount importance of nurturing a positive work milieu. Galvanized by these revelations, Alex initiated a meditation practice and actively advocated for team members to follow suit.

With the passage of time, a notable transformation rippled through the workplace ambiance. Collaboration among team members surged, communication became enhanced and creativity blossomed. Employees experienced a heightened sense of being valued and bolstered, culminating in elevated engagement levels and heightened productivity. As Alex persisted in fostering a sense of purpose and interconnection, the positive repercussions transcended the confines of the workplace, permeating into personal spheres of life.

In the journey of leadership, the integration of epigenetics and spirituality offers a profound paradigm shift. Understanding the power of our choices and the influence of the environment on gene expression empowers leaders to create a nurturing and harmonious workplace. Spirituality as a guiding force helps leaders tap into their authentic selves, fostering empathy, compassion and vision.

There is growing evidence that epigenetics, spirituality and leadership are all interconnected. For example, studies have shown that people who have a strong sense of purpose are more likely to have healthy epigenetic profiles. Additionally, meditation has been shown to have epigenetic effects, and can also help improve leadership skills.

Following Nelson Mandela's Example

Another story that illustrates the connection between epigenetics, spirituality and leadership is that of Nelson Mandela, the South African anti-apartheid revolutionary, political leader and philanthropist. He served as the first African-origin president of his country, from 1994 to 1999, and was the first head of state elected in a fully representative democratic election.

Mandela was imprisoned for twenty-seven years for his political activities under the apartheid regime. During his time in prison, he developed a strong sense of purpose and spirituality. He also learned to meditate, which helped him cope with the harsh conditions of prison life.[1]

After his release from prison, Mandela became a leader in the fight against apartheid. He was able to unite people from different backgrounds and cultures, and inspired them to work together for a common goal. Mandela's leadership was based on his strong sense of purpose and his commitment to non-violence.

Mandela's story shows how epigenetics, spirituality and leadership can all play a role in shaping our lives. It also shows how these factors can be used to create positive changes in the world.

The field of epigenetics is still relatively new, but it is rapidly growing. As we learn more about epigenetics, we are beginning to understand how our environment can have a profound impact on our genes. This knowledge can help us to make healthier choices and live more fulfilling lives.

Neuroplasticity and Arjuna's Archery Lesson

Within the Mahabharata, the tale of Arjuna's archery lesson serves as a vivid embodiment of the concept of neuroplasticity, showcasing the transformative potential embedded in focused practice and unyielding determination.

Dronacharya, the esteemed teacher, is conducting archery lessons for the Kuru princes, including the Pandavas and Kauravas, among whom is Arjuna, known for his exceptional talent.

To assess his students' focus and clarity of mind, Dronacharya positions a wooden bird high up in a tree and asks each prince, in turn, what they see.

Various responses are given, describing the complete scene, including the bird, the tree, and even surrounding elements like the sky and leaves. Whereas Arjuna responded by stating that he only sees the bird's eye.

Dronacharya praises Arjuna's single-minded focus, highlighting its importance in mastering archery and, metaphorically, in achieving success in life.

This story encapsulates the essence of neuroplasticity, showcasing the mind's remarkable malleability to disciplined practice and unwavering determination. Through Arjuna's journey, the tale underscores the profound capabilities of the human mind, where focused attention and dedication possess the power to sculpt neural pathways, elevate concentration and unlock extraordinary feats of achievement.

Through dedicated practice and unyielding determination, Arjuna had reshaped his neural connections, refining his mind to exclude distractions and attain a state of 'flow'—heightened concentration and absorption—allowing him to see only the bird's eye, and hit it with unerring accuracy.

It is a profound lesson about the potency of focus, determination and the boundless potential of the mind to achieve greatness. It serves as a reminder that the mind stands as a powerful, malleable instrument, which can be refined through disciplined practice and unwavering attentiveness.

Neuroplasticity is a concept that contemporary science has only recently begun to decipher. But like Arjuna, we can harness its potential to enhance our skills, surmount challenges and unlock our utmost potential in the relentless pursuit of excellence.

DKS and the Link to Neuroplasticity

The principles of dharma, karma and swadharma hold deep roots in ancient Eastern philosophies and spiritual traditions. While their fundamental purpose is to guide individuals towards ethical living and spiritual evolution, their influence can transcend spiritual realms, affecting diverse aspects of well-being, including the phenomenon of neuroplasticity.

Dharma embodies the concept of living in harmony with one's higher purpose and moral obligations. Embracing it entails making ethical decisions, acting with integrity and contributing positively to society. Engaging in purpose-driven living and upholding ethical principles have been associated with reduced stress levels and heightened emotional well-being, factors that can invariably influence neuroplasticity. Individuals who live in alignment with their dharma often experience a profound sense of fulfilment and contentment, leading to positive emotional states that can amplify neural connections associated with well-being and resilience.

Karma elucidates cause and effect, suggesting that our actions reverberate and shape our future. Engaging in positive actions and fostering kindness, empathy and compassion contribute to an emotionally nurturing environment. Such conduct nurtures robust social bonds, which improves neuroplasticity. Acts of kindness and compassion can trigger the release of neurochemicals like oxytocin and dopamine, fostering feelings of well-being and interconnectedness. These neurochemical dynamics can influence brain plasticity, fortifying constructive neural pathways related to empathy and emotional regulation.

Swadharma entails embracing one's inherent talents and unique calling. By discovering and aligning with their Swadharma, individuals often encounter a sense of authenticity and personal advancement. Engaging in activities that resonate with innate aptitude can lead to a state of 'flow'—as explained before, this means heightened concentration and absorption. Experiences of 'flow' have been correlated with shifts in brain function that stimulate heightened neuroplasticity. Engaging consistently in pursuits that induce 'flow' states can elevate cognitive faculties and innovation, potentially fostering enhanced neuroplasticity.

Adhering to dharma, practicing benevolent karma, and embracing swadharma can cumulatively contribute to stress reduction and improved emotional regulation. Prolonged stress has been shown to impede neuroplasticity and brain vitality.

Incorporating practices that alleviate stress, such as heartfulness meditation and introspection, can trigger neuroplastic alterations that strengthen neural pathways linked to emotional regulation and resilience.

While the direct influence of DKS on neuroplasticity is a multifaceted realm of exploration, persuasive correlations exist between these principles and myriad factors that impact the brain. Leading a life that aligns with one's higher calling, practicing affirmative deeds, discovering and nurturing innate talents, and diminishing stress through spiritual practices can collectively contribute to enhanced emotional well-being and cognitive prowess.

It's imperative to note that neuroplasticity remains the subject of ongoing research, but the age-old wisdom encapsulated by dharma, karma and swadharma furnishes a profound framework for personal evolution and self-unveiling, potentially influencing neuroplasticity and enriching overall well-being.

Purpose Over Power/Profit: The History of Manuneethi Chozhan

There is an incident in the Periya Puranam that explains an event that happened in the life of the Chozha king who became known as Manuneethi Chozhan because of the glorious justice he kept imparting and the values he espoused and lived for.

This exemplifies the impartial judicial practice the ruler, the ruling establishment or an organization should follow. When the king is that involved in upholding justice in spirit and action, irrespective of the personal agony he would suffer, people will live in love, and the land will prosper.

This king was born into the solar tradition of the Chozhas. He lived as a beacon of light and soul for all living beings in his realm. He appeased the forces of nature through numerous rituals and dedicated significant resources to the worship of deities. He also remained free of enemies, and came to be known as the 'Chozha of Justice'.

A son was born to him, described as having courage akin to a lion cub. The son was also skilled in various arts, a paragon of discipline, and adorned with numerous lovable traits. The king felt immense pride in his beloved son, watching him mature into a youth deserving of the title of prince.

One day, the king's young son was driving his chariot through the main roads of the capital, accompanied by his friends and forces. Unexpectedly, a calf wandered on to the road. Tragically, the creature was struck and killed by the chariot's wheel. The sight of the grieving mother cow, licking, crying and mourning by the side of the dead calf, struck the king's son deeply.

Overwhelmed by the incident, the prince sought solace through penance, feeling that he would tarnish his father's reputation as a champion of justice. Meanwhile, the grief-stricken cow made her way to the palace and tugged on the bell rope with her mouth—a customary way to request the king's intervention for justice. Rushing to the scene, the king saw the weeping cow and was informed by a knowledgeable minister about the calf's demise beneath the prince's chariot. Grief-stricken, the king was unable to bear the sight of the mourning cow and sat down, troubled. He inquired of his ministers how he could make amends for the tragic event.

The ministers suggested that his son should undergo the penance that Vedic scholars prescribed for such an incident. However, the king, who didn't merely adhere to justice for the sake of it, but deeply ingrained its essence into his rule, was displeased with this solution. He questioned the fairness of treating his son differently when he would not spare anyone else who took a life. He believed that it was his responsibility to ensure the protection of all lives in his kingdom, even if they were his own family members. Rejecting the idea of creating a separate rule for his son, he stood firm on upholding the principles of justice.

The ministers, citing the established practice of penance for such sins, persisted in their advice. The king, agitated by their response, exclaimed: 'You fail to grasp the spirit and truth behind justice. A grave sin has been committed by taking the life of a creature associated with the holy abode of Lord Shiva in my capital, Thiruvarur. To atone for this, my son must meet the same fate as the calf.'

The ministers were shaken, but the king ordered a minister's son to carry out the task of running over his son with a chariot. Refusing to perform such an act, the minister's son tragically took his own life.

Unswayed by the fact that his son was the only heir to the throne, the king himself took charge of the chariot, and ran over him. His subjects mourned the heir but appreciated the king's commitment to justice. As if responding to the divine call of justice, Lord Shiva appeared on the horizon, and the king paid his respects. The Lord blessed the king for his unwavering commitment to justice. Through divine grace, the calf, the king's son, and the minister's son were restored to life. Both the cow and the king found relief from their suffering.

The life and leadership of Manuneethi Chozhan offer lessons that transcend cultures and generations, resonating with leaders across time. He exemplified several enduring values of leadership, even though as the king, he could have wielded power without restraint.

He represented a leader who personified justice and fairness, battled against injustice even when it involved his own son, prioritized the well-being of creatures above all else, exhibited profound wisdom in governance, and above all, 'walked the talk' and led by example.

Through the embodiment of these principles and the practice of wise leadership, we can endeavour to make a positive and enduring impact in our roles as leaders. The legacy of Manuneethi Chozhan has persevered through centuries, inspiring generations with his leadership attributes and dedication to justice. It serves as a reminder that our actions and influence as leaders can extend far beyond our tenure.

Constructing a positive legacy through ethical leadership and consequential choices ensures that our influence will continue to inspire others for many years to come. While the concept of prioritizing purpose over profit may seem contemporary, the kings of bygone eras, including those from several centuries ago, lived by these values, which have withstood the test of time.

Power of Perspective and Leadership Play

Perspectives are potent. They possess the potential to profoundly shape an individual's approach to leadership and cognitive processes.

They function as lenses through which individuals perceive the world, interpret situations and take decisions. These lenses are moulded by experiences, beliefs, values, culture and personal biases. Acknowledging and harnessing the diverse perspectives that encompass a leader's sphere can pave the way for more efficacious leadership and inventive thinking.

Let us delve into the Mahabharata once again, and immerse ourselves in yet another tale to enhance our comprehension. This narrative centres around Ekalavya, a young tribal archer, whose journey epitomizes the far-reaching influence of both perspectives and leadership dynamics.

Ekalavya's narrative commences with his unswerving aspiration to master archery under the tutelage of the revered Guru Dronacharya, the mentor of the Kuru princes. Yet, Ekalavya is considered 'low-born', and his quest to approach Dronacharya is met with rejection due to his social status. Undeterred, Ekalavya sculpts a likeness of Dronacharya from clay, and vows to hone his archery skills by practicing before this statue.

As Ekalavya's dedication and proficiency develop, he metamorphoses into a remarkable archer in his own right. His perspective evolves from the pursuit of external validation to the mastery of his craft for personal growth. Here, we are witness to the potential potency of an exceptional perspective that diverges from the conventional. Ekalavya's self-reliance and unwavering commitment to his objectives illuminate the notion that leadership can emanate not solely from formal mentorship, but also from intrinsic resolve.

Unexpectedly, the narrative takes a twist when a dog, wandering near the Kuru palace, chances upon Ekalavya's practice area. Intrigued by the distinctive sound of arrows hitting their mark, the dog approaches Ekalavya. Remarkably proficient, Ekalavya shoots arrows to silence the dog's barking without causing it harm.

This incident, witnessed by Arjuna, one of Dronacharya's esteemed disciples, introduces a multifaceted perspective on leadership. While admiring Ekalavya's prowess, Arjuna perceives him as a potential adversary. Fearing competition, Arjuna returns to Dronacharya and voices his apprehensions. Dronacharya, aware of Ekalavya's identity, devises a strategy to protect Arjuna's standing.

Dronacharya approaches Ekalavya and demands an agonizing price as his guru dakshina (teacher's fee). Ekalavya's unwavering devotion prompts him to acquiesce without hesitation. Dronacharya insists on Ekalavya surrendering his right thumb, effectively stripping him of his archery prowess.

Ekalavya's perspective undergoes a dramatic shift, transitioning from one of self-improvement and self-reliance to disillusionment with a system that enforced limitations based on societal constructs like caste.

This story encapsulates the intricate interplay between perspectives and leadership. Ekalavya's journey—from being denied mentorship to evolving into a self-taught virtuoso—underscores the potential potency of an unconventional perspective. Concurrently, Arjuna's perception of Ekalavya as a threat underscores the impact of rivalry and comparison within leadership dynamics. Dronacharya's decision, propelled by his wish to sustain his favoured disciple's supremacy, unveils the intricacies that underlie leadership and authority.

Ultimately, Ekalavya's tale becomes an admonitory parable, urging leaders to weigh the ethical ramifications of their choices, and to recognize the potential repercussions of manipulating perspectives to preserve power. His journey underscores that leadership transcends hierarchical structures. The essence of true leadership lies in nurturing individual development, fostering diverse perspectives and making decisions that prioritize the collective good over personal gain.

In Ekalavya's sacrifice and Arjuna's envy, we discern reflections of the complexities that define leadership within the Mahabharata—an epic that transcends temporal, cultural and geographical boundaries to proffer invaluable insights into the intricate interplay of perspectives and leadership dynamics.

Minority Leadership

I hail from a background deeply engaged with corporate affairs, CEOs and executives, constituting a substantial portion of my professional endeavours. My work is predominantly centred within this realm. One of the most coveted forms of assistance sought by individuals pertains to leadership development, a critical requirement for virtually every organization.

Be it within the context of spirituality, organizational structures, nations or the global arena, the ultimate goal consistently revolves around the welfare of the majority. Throughout the annals of history, it becomes apparent that those who stand to benefit the most—often constituting the majority—rarely possess a clear understanding of their actual needs. Nevertheless, there exists a persistent misconception that the majority perspective is inherently correct.

Four centuries ago, it was widely held that the earth beneath our feet was flat, and that the entire cosmos revolved around us. This belief in the earth's flatness was upheld by the majority viewpoint for numerous millennia. However, the concept of a spherical Earth originated with the ancient Greeks, and it was figures like Pythagoras and Aristotle who provided early evidence and reasoning to support this theory. While Galileo played a significant role in advocating for heliocentrism (the Sun-centered model) in the sixteenth century, which faced significant opposition, the understanding of the Earth's curvature predates him by over two millennia.

What does this indicate?

We initiate our journey from home. In childhood, parents instil values and impose restrictions, guiding us through a world we are yet to fully understand. While their decisions may at times feel restrictive, it is important to remember that they often hold the unpopular opinion of what is best for us in the long run.

Consider Indian history as well. Inspired by a resolute conviction, Mahatma Gandhi returned to India and tirelessly spearheaded the non-cooperation movement. While Gandhi's leadership and vision were undeniably crucial, it's important to recognize that the movement flourished through the collective effort of countless individuals. The Indian National Congress, along with millions of dedicated supporters, played a vital role in achieving independence. Throughout the struggle, Gandhi embodied the maxim 'what I stand for is a cause worth standing for', demonstrating unwavering commitment to the movement's goals. His journey, though marked by immense hardships, was ultimately successful as people increasingly rallied around him and his vision, recognizing the path towards freedom and emancipation.

Even at the most basic level of collective action, individuals with materialistic priorities might prioritize self-preservation and the status quo, aiming for stability and personal gain. However, when leaders call for change, resistance arises from the natural human tendency to preserve comfort and routine. Discomfort can be a powerful deterrent, even though it might be the catalyst for personal and societal transformation. Convincing people to step outside their comfort zones and contribute to collective action, even when it requires individual sacrifices, remains a significant challenge. While some may passively wait for change to happen on its own, effective leadership focuses on addressing concerns, fostering collective purpose, and offering a compelling vision for the future.

Remarkably, despite a population of around 300 million, several individuals across India contributed in various ways to the freedom movement. While it's impossible to determine the exact number of participants due to the diverse forms of involvement, their collective efforts played a significant role in achieving independence.

Hence, the central intent of this book resides in reshaping your existing belief system that subscribes to the notion that the 'majority is right'; to challenge convictions that profitability is the sole business imperative, and similar others. To challenge the notion that 'if we abstain, others will act in the future; if we decline cooperation, others will seize the opportunity and reap benefits'.

The majority is naturally inclined to resist change. However, when change becomes imperative, the onus falls on the minority to catalyse it into a movement, a principle elucidated by the life stories of the history's renowned change-makers.

The question that confronts us here is whether we desire to align ourselves with that minority that endeavours to challenge the prevailing belief system in our world. Regardless of whether you maintain such a belief or not, do you wish to be part of the change that is inevitably bound to unfold?

Leaders, while occupying singular positions, often strive to embody and represent the collective aspirations or best interests of a larger group.

This dynamic can also be applied to negative forces. Figures like Adolf Hitler, despite representing a small group, were able to manipulate and exploit societal anxieties to gain power. While it's important to acknowledge the dangers of such figures, it's crucial to remember that Germany was not prospering at the time of Hitler's rise. The country was grappling with the aftermath of World War I, burdened by economic hardship and political instability.

The pivotal query becomes: If goodness is to triumph over malevolence, if values are to take precedence and guide the world, then the responsibility lies with us—do we choose to rise to the occasion or not? The decision rests in our hands. In a struggle between good and evil, initially, good will invariably find itself in the minority. The challenge becomes how to expand its influence. How can the propagation of the much-needed goodness be effectively ensured?

Within every historical lesson, scientific insight and even any instance of transformative change, there exists a concept known as the tipping point, a juncture beyond which there is no return, or critical mass has been achieved.

Malcolm Gladwell's famous 2000 book, titled *Tipping Point*, explores the idea that this is the critical moment when an idea, trend or social behaviour crosses a threshold and spreads rapidly, leading to a significant change or transformation. Gladwell explores through real-world examples how certain phenomena reach a tipping point and, as we have come to understand it, go 'viral', and the various factors that contribute to this. The book analyses the dynamics of social epidemics and how small actions or changes can lead to disproportionate and widespread effects.

For many religions that now have a large following, it took a significant amount of time to reach widespread adoption. In ancient times, the spread of religious teachings primarily relied on word-of-mouth communication, which presented considerable challenges. This stands in stark contrast to the modern communication landscape where information can be disseminated rapidly and widely through various technologies.

Lord Krishna's explanation to Arjuna by way of the Bhagavad Gita is profoundly insightful. 'Who are you to release the arrow? They are already destined to perish. If you abstain, the task will still be accomplished. You have an opportunity to shoot, through which you can claim the credit for victory in this Mahabharata.' After those 700 verses, Arjuna comprehends the truth, wages war and wins.

This truth remains applicable till the present day. Every one of us embodies an Arjuna, if given a chance. For Krishna, employing his Sudarshan chakra would have swiftly ended the conflict. Bhishma persistently challenged Krishna throughout the war, until the tenth day, when fell and lay on his bed of arrows. He implored: 'Please, Krishna, I wish not to meet my end by another's hand. Employ your chakra and conclude my existence.' Numerous narratives attest to his fervent appeal, stemming from his aspiration for the most elevated death.

If someone must undertake the task of ushering change, what then is Arjuna's role, or by extension, our role? Are we merely observers as Lord Krishna wages war? Unbeknownst to us, we contribute to change by altering our households and local environments. Nevertheless, a distinction exists between the eating habits of a child and an adult. A child consumes without conscious choice, guided by the parent. Adults are selective, and mindful of the changes they bring about.

The moment has come for us to embrace the unwavering belief that every individual possesses the potential to instigate profound transformation in this world. This is our true calling.

What Human Mind Can Conceive and Believe, It Can Achieve

The sections above are meant to help the reader introspect on some questions that earlier chapters might have left unanswered. They also help put this book in perspective—whatever the human mind can conceive and consistently believe, it can achieve.

This statement underscores the power of belief and positive thinking in shaping human potential and accomplishment. This concept highlights the idea that our thoughts and beliefs have a profound influence on our actions, decisions and outcomes. If we can visualize and maintain unwavering faith in our goals and aspirations, we are more likely to take the necessary steps and overcome obstacles to turn those visions into reality. This mindset aligns with phenomena like self-fulfilling prophecies and the law of attraction, where our thoughts and beliefs attract corresponding experiences and results.

12

A Bird's Eye View

Long ago, possibly around the third century BCE, a wise king embarked on a mission to enlighten his three young sons about the intricate ways of the world.

The king commissioned a sagacious Brahmin named Vishnu Sharma to educate his sons. Renowned for his storytelling gift, Vishnu Sharma embarked on the task of imparting invaluable lessons to the princes through fables and animal-centric tales, having explained his approach to the king beforehand.

This collection of tales was the *Panchatantra*—a title that translates to 'five guiding principles'. It consists not just of standalone stories, but also intriguing interwoven narratives, leading from one story to the next, to enhance comprehension. This approach aimed to not just entertain the young royals, but also instil within them lasting moral and ethical insights.

As time progressed, the princes derived not only enjoyment from these captivating narratives, but also began to decipher the profound meanings and lessons hidden beneath the surface. They discerned the applicability of these tales in their own lives, and in the governance of a kingdom. The once-young heirs eventually ascended to become accomplished kings and 'CEOs', fortified by the moral and ethical wisdom acquired from these stories.

Themes spanning governance, friendship, loyalty, deceit, love, wisdom and decision-making were adeptly woven into the fabric of these tales.

A distinctive facet of the *Panchatantra* is that the narratives frequently employ wit, humour and ingenious plot twists, captivating audiences while conveying moral insights. These fables leverage metaphors, allegories and symbolism to convey profound meanings, prompting introspection.

Globally, storytelling is an ancient and potent tradition that has enthralled audiences throughout history. While its medium has evolved and diversified, its essence remains timeless. It's an art that has been passed down across generations, shaping cultures and forging deep connections between people. Even today, storytelling remains a pivotal tool across diverse spheres such as literature, theatre (both cinematic and non-cinematic), marketing, news and public speaking. What accounts for the resounding impact of storytelling, and why is it hailed as an art form?

Storytelling yields a profound influence on the brain, fostering the acceleration of cognitive processes. When we engage with a story, multiple regions of our brain activate, encompassing those responsible for language processing, sensory perception and emotional responses. This intricate activation renders the experience more immersive and unforgettable, compared to mere presentation of facts or information. The potential of storytelling to create accessible memory recall is particularly evident in modern news presentation formats, where information is often presented in narrative form.

The concept of spiritual storytelling within the context of modern business life involves the integration of spiritual and ethical principles into narratives that not only inspire, but also guide and mould the organizational culture. This practice encompasses the use of stories to establish a connection between individuals and deeper layers of meaning, purpose and values within the framework of their work and professional domains.

Storytelling stands as a potent tool for management due to its capacity to captivate, invigorate and motivate employees. By employing the power of storytelling, managers can foster engagement throughout the entire spectrum, linking employees to the organization's overarching vision and mission. This two-way interaction enhances communication channels and promotes a positive and productive work atmosphere.

While these endeavours contribute to shaping a collective culture within groups, a parallel necessity exists to instil values at the individual leadership level. The achievement of a comprehensive 360-degree viewpoint is facilitated by a unifying narrative that encompasses all aspects. For instance, in our organization, DEXIAN, we are deeply engaged with the concept of business for good. Our employees participate in the DRISE programme, ensuring that their individual contributions toward society, beyond organizational KPIs, are aligned, thereby reinforcing their commitment to building the brand.

Indian mythology represents a reservoir of wisdom and life lessons that hold applicability across diverse realms, including business and leadership. Gandhi's transformation into the revered 'Mahatma' was catalysed by a life-altering encounter with the tale of King Harishchandra. Even in contemporary times, numerous CEOs turn to the Bhagavad Gita for inspiration and elevated philosophical contemplation. The Gita, a profound discourse by Lord Krishna to Arjuna on the battlefield, continues to exert its influence due to its ability to provide compelling insights into life's core aspects from the very crucible of conflict.

While adherence to dharma tales is not obligatory for Indian CEOs, a multitude of individuals across the country draw insight from mythology and cultural values. Dharma tales, enriched with intricate symbolism and instructive narratives, offer guidance and perspectives that can significantly impact leaders in their professional and personal capacities.

Within the Indian context, the principles of dharma—encompassing righteousness, duty and moral obligations—hold profound cultural significance. Any CEOs who align their actions with these principles are often regarded as leaders who champion ethics, integrity and social responsibility.

By assimilating the wisdom inherent in Indian dharma tales into their decision-making processes and leadership styles, Indian CEOs can resonate with the societal ethos and values that underpin the environment they operate within. In many cases, these principles reside within the hearts of individuals, even without deliberate reading, serving as a foundation for their successful journeys.

In a broader context, regardless of religious affiliation, the narratives found in sacred texts like the Bible, the Quran, the Hadith, Jain Agama Sutras, Buddhist Jataka tales, Zen stories, the Ramayana and the Mahabharata share a common theme—they collectively offer insights into ethical dilemmas, challenges in leadership and the imperative of balancing material success with spiritual and societal well-being.

Then, there are works like the *Arabian Nights*, the collection of middle-Eastern folktales compiled during the Islamic golden age. The framing device of these tales Stories like 'Aladdin's Wonderful Lamp', 'Ali Baba and the Forty Thieves' and 'Sinbad the Sailor' have become closely associated with the Arabian Nights collection, exemplifying its themes of triumph over evil, adventure, and rich storytelling. While these tales weren't part of the original One Thousand and One Nights canon, they were added in later translations—often inspired by Middle Eastern folklore—and quickly gained popularity worldwide.

That Scheherazade's storytelling could sway the king to suspend a death sentence underscores intriguing facets of human psychology, like our inherent attraction to narratives.

The crux of the Vikram and Betaal stories in the *Betaal Pachisi* is to convey moral and ethical principles. Each narrative frequently introduces a moral quandary, an ethical choice, or a lesson touching upon justice, honesty, loyalty, or the repercussions of one's actions. These stories are designed to engage the listener or reader in critical thinking, and evoke contemplation about morality.

The tales of Vikram and Betaal prompt listeners and readers to ponder the ramifications of their decisions and deeds. They underline the significance of sagacity, honesty and ethical choices, even in arduous circumstances. These narratives often underscore the supremacy of knowledge, intellect and moral discernment in surmounting obstacles and resolving dilemmas. The tales furnish CEOs with exemplars of virtuous characters who embody qualities like honesty, compassion, humility and altruism.

Similarly, this book seeks to cultivate values among CEOs through various stories. In essence, it endeavours to craft a narrative that employs storytelling in a manner that engages and resonates with the audience. Beyond mere dissemination of information, it delves into the realm of emotions, imagination and human experiences. Furthermore, it introduces intriguing inquiries about the stories themselves, offering the author's perspectives on incidents and characters. This approach imparts fresh viewpoints to readers.

Each chapter is impeccably organized, featuring six well-defined sub-topics. A concise synopsis serves as an inspiring preamble for the chapter, accompanied by a note on the source of that inspiration. This unique approach aims to serve as a catalyst, urging readers to probe further. The author intentionally avoids confining readers' contemplation solely to his book; he encourages them to venture beyond its confines and explore the origins that sparked the ideas. Rather than merely imparting instructions, the intention of a book should be to kindle inspiration that propels individuals beyond their existing perceptions.

A prelude to each topic extends the initial inspiration into actionable insights. For a skilled storyteller, this prelude becomes a crucial tool to build momentum, stoking curiosity within readers' minds. Should a reader's attention waver during the chapter despite the prelude, a set of rapid-fire questions emerges to reignite interest and transition to the next stage. At this juncture, readers have matured enough to grasp the direction the author intends to guide them in. Acknowledging that the human mind cannot indefinitely absorb instructions while retaining comprehension, the introduction of a connected narrative infuses interest and ensures a comprehensive grasp of the chapter's content.

Once the assimilation of copious information is underway, a conclusive summary and actionable points wrap up the chapter. This transition from what is anticipated to what can be gleaned from the chapter renders the book not only captivating, but also tremendously informative. The carefully crafted structure invites readers to embark on an engaging and enriching reading experience that transcends mere consumption of content.

As for the chapters, they have different teachings to impart.

'Vision and Corporate Karma', drawn from the Mahabharata, navigates a two-directional path—one peering into the future, the other actively shaping the future through the prism of past actions. The tale of Bhishma serves as an illuminating illustration of karma and its unforeseen consequences. What stands out is that the karma of an enterprise extends not only to the organizational level, but also deeply influences individuals. The collective karma, as well as the karma of the CEO, exerts a sweeping impact on the enterprise as an integrated entity.

'Strategic Thinking and Dharma', inspired by the Mahabharata, delves into a pivotal facet of the cognitive process. Contrasting with many management guides that commence with perception, this discourse underlines that the foundation lies in thoughtful contemplation. The essence of this thinking should align with dharma, for without it, the entire endeavour is futile. An analogous narrative surfaces in Bhishma's perspective of eliminating the Pandavas—a notion eventually invalidated due to its misalignment. Even a mind of profound acumen couldn't execute its intent, as highlighted through the interactions of Krishna, Bhishma, and the eventual victory of the Pandavas.

'Steadfast Execution and Personal Accountability', sourced from the Mahabharata, prompts a significant query. Although execution garners immense attention at the group level, accountability is inherently individualistic. The case of Abhimanyu and the Chakravyuha poses an intriguing conundrum. The plans of both the Kauravas and the Pandavas faltered. The Kauravas executed their group strategy, achieving partial success in Abhimanyu's demise. However, their overarching objective of capturing Yudhishthira was thwarted due to Abhimanyu's unwavering personal accountability. Hence, true success necessitates a marriage of collective execution and individual responsibility within the group. When one exhibits dedication and personal accountability, the fruits manifest in unwavering group execution.

As the book advances, it introduces a range of concepts in subsequent chapters: communication, selflessness, spiritual quotient, humility, purpose (or, as the Japanese call it, 'ikigai'), empathy, high values and integrity. These concepts are sourced from various sacred texts, adding a layer of authenticity and tapping into past experiences for the readers' benefit. Enriching the narrative are stories like 'The Maharishi and the Dog', 'King Shibi and the Dove', Sahadeva's prescience, Arjuna's hubris, and Duryodhana's demise. These stories not only recount familiar tales but also offer fresh perspectives, breathing new life into well-known narratives. The journey through these concepts provides an emphatic insight into one's responsibilities towards oneself, the immediate surroundings and the broader purpose one serves.

A pivotal understanding emerges—maintaining a state of equanimity within the mind, unwavering and unperturbed. This concept finds poignant resonance in the tale of 'The Maharishi and a Dog', narrated by none other than rishi Narada when the Pandavas were living incognito. Shedding egos, identities and power allows one to grasp life's true essence—a practice embodied by the Pandavas, and essential for CEOs.

Yudhishthira's enquiry about a king's life leads Narada to elucidate that his responsibility extends beyond mere actions; it encompasses even thoughts. Communication, both explicit and implicit, is a vital facet, reflecting the king's duty to uphold the dharma of the group, and the swadharma of individuals. Clear, respectful communication fosters clarity and a balanced mindset among those carrying out the king's directives. This understanding aligns with the overarching journey of the book's chapters.

Once the king, or a modern-day CEO, adeptly navigates shedding ego and identity for collective goals, and communicates through actions and thoughts, the exploration of altruism ensues. Altruism signifies selflessly advocating for the welfare of others. The story of Shibi, who safeguards an ordinary dove from a hawk's clutches, epitomizes the empathy a king/CEO should extend even to non-human subjects within their realm. But while safeguarding one aspect, the potential repercussions on other groups need prudent management. A king/CEO must orchestrate equilibrium while safeguarding diverse stakeholders. Amid the prevalent urge to prioritize profit above all, the chapter on altruism or selflessness posits that CEOs may need to relinquish personal gains. Shibi's story, which balances the needs of hawks and doves, intricately presents harmony among various stakeholders, illustrating the ability to selflessly pursue a collective cause.

As learning expands beyond organizational growth, it becomes imperative to fathom one's Spiritual Quotient—the capacity to comprehend and connect with life's deeper meanings and purposes for both oneself and the organization. This involves establishing profound connections with others, cultivating self-awareness while fostering awareness among those connected, and recognizing the interrelatedness with the world at large. The tale of Sahadeva, the all-knowing, resonates here. His ability to bind even Lord Krishna himself underscores his capacity to influence outcomes. However, he harnessed this knowledge to serve the grand cosmic design orchestrated by the Lord. Building awareness about the underlying reasons behind certain behaviours proves crucial for a CEO's journey, echoing Sahadeva's approach. The key learning lies not in attempting to control everything, but in grasping that certain events are bound to unfold naturally. This theme is elegantly amplified in the chapter titled 'The Interplay of Spiritual Quotient and Organizational Growth', highlighting how the reader's understanding is enriched by absorbing the essence of SQ while fostering environmental awareness.

The subsequent chapter naturally revolves around the most eminent warrior of the Mahabharata—Arjuna. Despite his profound understanding of divinity through Krishna's personal tutelage, and remarkable accomplishments on the battlefield, Arjuna's humility and groundedness faltered when Krishna instructed him to disembark his chariot post-war. This deficiency hindered Arjuna from gleaning life's lessons fully, notwithstanding his boundless triumphs. In this context, the absence of humility and a sense of groundedness stands as an admonition for CEOs, signifying that these traits can swiftly erode success. The initial passage offers intriguing introspection: 'He who possesses humility and a sense of groundedness, for whom a piece of stone (criticism) and gold (appreciation) are equal.'

As the final chapter took shape, it seemed unfair to exclusively spotlight individuals of exemplary character. Life is replete with shades of grey, and this chapter delves into that realm. Duryodhana comes to the fore in 'Guided by a Larger Purpose/Cause—The Unsolved Mysteries'.

In the story, Duryodhana's vision was limited to his own tactical wins, failing to grasp the broader purpose or cause. Leadership transcends mere victories; it entails comprehending the ramifications of unsolved mysteries.

When a cause we support is potentially tainted by self-interest, what considerations should we make in deciding how to engage or distance ourselves?

Irrespective of leadership tactics, selfish objectives culminate in opposing outcomes. Despite being a great warrior with a formidable army and skilled generals, Duryodhana faced reversals he couldn't accept, embodying leadership's failure to grasp the environment, and imposing self-centred aims.

A parallel account is offered through Karna's story in 'High on Values and Integrity: Dharma vs Swadharma'. 'Karna's Last Temptation' tells the story of how this warrior, despite Lord Krishna's request to reveal his identity a week prior to the war, succumbed to temptation and refrained from disclosure. He chose self-sacrifice, ensuring the protection of his brothers who stood for dharma by vowing not to harm them. Prioritizing the cause above personal gain reflects true greatness, exemplifying a CEO's virtue in every thought and action. The narrative culminates with even Lord Krishna beseeching Karna, underscoring the remarkable impact of selflessness.

'Yaksha Prashna' is an intriguing narrative centred on a Q&A between a father and son—the disguised Yama and Yudhishthira. The importance of maintaining mental clarity even in adversity is vividly demonstrated by Yudhishthira, while his younger brothers lie dead on the ground. This quality exemplifies a paramount attribute of a virtuous leader. Furthermore, when presented with the choice to revive one of his fallen brothers, Yudhishthira's choice of Nakula underscores his empathetic connection with the individuals under his leadership.

This chapter delves into profound inquiries concerning life, duty, ethics and the underlying nature of reality. Yudhishthira's responses are grounded in a singular truth—the impermanence of human existence. Despite the constant departures of those around us, people often cling to the illusion of their own permanence. This perspective fosters humility coupled with empathy, traits that hold great significance for a CEO, especially considering the multitude of families reliant on their decisions and actions.

In conclusion to this chapter, two renowned quotes are rekindled in my mind. Swami Vivekananda's 'moral stories have the power to ignite the conscience and awaken the dormant virtues within us', and Rabindranath Tagore's 'in the realm of moral stories, we find the gems of life's lessons that help us navigate the complexities of the world'.

I extend my heartfelt congratulations to S. Prakash, the corporate sage, for presenting these invaluable life lessons in a narrative form, tailored for modern-day corporate CEOs. I am confident that readers will greatly benefit from incorporating these principles into their personal, professional and business endeavours.

Kumar Rajagopalan
Vice president—international operations and
country head for India,
Dexian, DISYS India

Notes

6: The Interplay of Spiritual Quotient and Organizational Growth

1 Sahadeva, known for his extraordinary intelligence and foresight, possessed the gift of prophecy and strategic insight. However, Lord Krishna, foreseeing potential disruptions caused by Sahadeva's unwelcome revelations during critical junctures, imposed a divine decree upon him to maintain silence at such moments, ensuring smooth progression of events without unwarranted interruptions.

11: Baker's Dozen

1 Source: Nelson Mandela, *Long Walk to Freedom*, Back Bay Books, 1995, and various letters and speeches of Nelson Mandela.

About the Author

S. Prakash, also known as Corporate Sage, is founder and CEO, SEE CHANGE Consulting, India. He is a widely read person and brings with him a rich blend of work, business, management, leadership and spiritual experience of more than four decades. He is a nationally acclaimed author, coach, master storyteller, keynote speaker, an organizational turnaround expert and nation-builder. He has been writing on human behaviour, business success and many other related topics for over two decades now. He has twelve books published to his credit (in several languages) and has authored over a thousand articles on self-development, spirituality and varied topics. He has over two thousand original quotations attributed to him.

Dharma Tales for CEOs is based on his understanding of Indian mythology, corporate life cycles and how they connect to the leadership and organizational shifts that are happening globally. He is an avid reader, has been practising Heartfulness Meditation since

1992 and is a certified Heartfulness trainer. Thanks to the various roles he plays in his corporate life and the Heartfulness Institute, he has a great exposure in interfacing with humans from across the world.

He is secretary to Daaji, the Global Guide who is the President of Heartfulness Institute.

HarperCollins *Publishers* India

At HarperCollins India, we believe in telling the best stories and finding the widest readership for our books in every format possible. We started publishing in 1992; a great deal has changed since then, but what has remained constant is the passion with which our authors write their books, the love with which readers receive them, and the sheer joy and excitement that we as publishers feel in being a part of the publishing process.

Over the years, we've had the pleasure of publishing some of the finest writing from the subcontinent and around the world, including several award-winning titles and some of the biggest bestsellers in India's publishing history. But nothing has meant more to us than the fact that millions of people have read the books we published, and that somewhere, a book of ours might have made a difference.

As we look to the future, we go back to that one word— a word which has been a driving force for us all these years.

Read.